Creative Jamaican Cooking & Menus

with Jerk, Barbecue and Selected Menus

GW00598663

By
Master C
Leonard 'Sonny' Henry
and
Mike Henry

LMH Publishing

Published by LMH Publishing Ltd.
7-9 Norman Road, Kingston CSO
Email: henryles@cwjamaica.com

Printed & Bound in Jamaica

ISBN 976-610-170-1

CONTENTS

Foreword

This is a cookbook devoted to people who delight in tasty, spicy food. The special sections on Barbecues and Menus will be a helpful aid to those who enjoy entertaining. The index also makes the book a useful reference for those interested in serious cuisine.

The recipes in the book reflect to a large extent the cultural heritage of the people in Jamaica: thus you will find recipes that reflect the Indian, African, European and both North and Latin American aspects of its culinary character following the Jamaican motto "Out Of May One People." Many of the dishes have been adapted to make use of the food we grow, such as ackee, plantain, coconut, paw-paw, mango, cassava and many others, which are considered exotic in other parts of the world.

For our foreign visitors who wish to prepare at home some of the dishes they may have tasted in restaurants or hotels, this book will be a handy guide. In many cases they will be able to find the ingredients they need in their local markets or West Indian communities.

For those who live here, may this book encourage a new and happy familiarity with foods we grow.

The Publishers

Appetizers & Hors d'oeuvres

OYSTERS

The best way to eat fresh oysters is raw. Open, and lay on a bed of crushed ice. Dress with lime juice. Brown bread and butter is usually served.

CURRIED CODFISH

½ lb. salt codfish
2 tablespoons minced onion
1 tablespoon curry powder

1 teaspoon lime juice
* flour
* oil

Wash fish, and cut into strips. Flour lightly and fry in bubbling oil. Take out the fish. Fry onion in the pan. Sprinkle with curry powder and moisten with lime juice. Allow to simmer, then add slices of fish and heat through. Serve on toast.

EGG PLANT ELEGANTE
(garden egg)

peeled egg plant
boiled crushed potatoes
salt, pepper, flour, oil

* chopped garlic (1 clove)
* vinegar and oil

Slice garden egg lengthwise into fingers. Season with salt and pepper and roll in flour. Drop into deep hot oil and fry until crisp.
Combine crushed potatoes, garlic and enough vinegar and oil to make a paste of dipping consistency. Place in a bowl and use fried egg plant fingers as scoops.

GRAPEFRUIT WITH SHRIMP
AND SOUR CREAM

½ grapefruit per person
6 shrimps, cooked and cleaned per
person

1 cup sour cream
1 tablespoon mayonnaise

Cut grapefruit in half. Core and remove pulp. Discard seeds.
Fill with cooked shrimps, marinated in sour cream and mayonnaise and mixed wi
grapefruit pulp.

PINEAPPLE APPETIZER

*   pieces of fresh pineapple
*   cream cheese

*   chopped cashew nuts

Dip pieces of pineapple in cheese and roll in cashews. Serve on too.hpicks.

COCONUT CHIPS

1 dry coconut

Remove meat from shell. Cut meat into thin strips and arrange in a shallow pa
Sprinkle with salt and toast in a slow oven. Stir occasionally.

FRIED PLANTAIN CHIPS

1 green plantain   *   oil

Peel plantain and cut into 1/6" thick slices. Fry in hot oil. Drain on paper towe
Sprinkle with salt to serve.

PORK RIND (SKIN)

*   whatever quantity desired
2-3 tablespoon oil

*   salt

Cut rind (skin) into small pieces and fry until crisp in oil. Sprinkle with salt.

COCO FRITTERS

cocos	* chopped escallion, salt pepper
tablespoon flour	1 egg
teaspoon baking powder	* oil

Wash and peel cocos. Grate and mix with other ingredients. Drop by spoonfuls into hot oil. When golden brown, remove and drain.

ACKEE WITH CHEESE

cups cooked ackees, crushed	1 tablespoon each butter, salt,
cups mild grated cheese	pepper

Mix all together, heat through and serve on toast.

NASSAU CAKE

tomatoes	1 tablespoon chopped onion
sweet peppers	* oil, salt, pepper
green or black olives	1 french type loaf of bread

Make this the day before it is to be used.

Chop tomatoes, peppers and olives. Add onion and seasoning. Cut bread in half lengthwise. Remove the crumbs and mix them into the tomato mixture, kneading it with a little oil, salt and pepper.

Fill the bread halves, and press together. Wrap in foil and refrigerate. Cut in slices to serve.

PEPPER SHRIMPS

pint of shrimps	½ sliced onion
white vinegar, water	* salt and pimento grains
sliced hot pepper (remove the seeds)	

Cover shrimps with salted water and boil until tender. Cool, peel and clean them. Meanwhile mix vinegar, peppers, onions and pimento grains. Bring to a boil Pour over shrimps and store in a covered jar for 12 hours before serving.

RIO COBRE MUD

1 chopped onion	3 tablespoons grated cheese
1 tablespoon butter	* creole sauce to taste
1 tin red pea soup	* a drop of hot sauce

Fry onion in butter. Add red pea soup and cheese. Stir over a low flame until cheese i melted.

Add sauces to taste and serve hot on slices of toast.

SEA URCHIN (Sea Eggs)

3 doz. sea eggs (not the black spiny type)

Wash well, open and remove the coral. This can be mixed with a white sauce a served on toast.

Sea eggs are considered a delicacy in many countries. The coral is scraped out a eaten raw with a squeeze of lemon or lime.

WATER MELON MARBLES

1 water melon	2 tablespoons sugar
¼ pint rum	* cherries
2 oranges	

Cut the melon in half lengthwise. Remove the seeds, then with a ball-scoop remov the flesh of the melon. The shell can be kept to be a serving dish if wished.

Place the melon balls in a bowl. Mix the rum, orange juice and sugar together a pour over the melon balls. Refrigerate for at least one hour.

To serve, place a cocktail stick in each ball and pile up on a bed of cracked ice the melon shell.

SEASONED BREADFRUIT CHIPS WITH
AVOCADO CREAM CHEESE DIP

readfruit Chips
  breadfruit
  salt
  black pepper

* onion salt
* garlic powder
* oil

Peel breadfruit, cut into sections and remove the heart. Cut into slices and place in alted water for half an hour or more. Dry the slices and fry in hot fat until golden. rain on paper towels. Meanwhile, mix the salt and seasonings together and sprinkle ver the chips just before serving.

vocado Cream Cheese Dip
  medium avocado pear
  ozs. cream cheese
  teaspoon minced onion

1 tablespoon lemon or lime juice
2 tablespoons milk
* salt

Halve avocado lengthwise and remove seed. Scoop out the pulp. The shell can be ved to be used as a container for serving, otherwise discard. Mash the pulp with cream heese and other ingredients. Serve piled in a small dish or the shell, surrounded by readfruit chips.

STAMP AND GO

The recipe for codfish fritters on page 11 makes a very popular cocktail snack when e fritters are made small and kept crisp. They can be served with the Avocado Dip ove or with a fish-flavoured dip.

TASTY JERK PORK BITES

lb. jerk pork
small onion
small country pepper

½ teaspoon powdered ginger
2 teaspoons Pickapeppa sauce
2 ozs. rum

Cut jerk pork into small pieces and place in blender. Remove seeds from country pper and place in blender with other ingredients. Blend until smooth. Chill.
Serve on small, bite-size crackers.

Soups

BAHAMIAN CONCH SOUP

1 cup of cooked and chopped conch
   meat which has been boiled in 1 qrt.
   of water
½ lb. diced tomatoes

½ lb. sliced onions
2 tablespoons oil
* herbs, garlic, salt to taste
* sherry optional

Heat oil and fry onions, tomatoes, and seasonings. Add these ingredients to con meat and liquid. Cook about 20 minutes.

1 teaspoon sherry is often added to this. Only the meat of the young queen con must be used.

CHOCHO PUREE

4 chochos peeled and diced
1 cup milk

* butter, herbs, salt, nutmeg to taste

Boil chocho until tender. Pour into blender with herbs and milk and blend un smooth. Reheat to serve with a dab of butter and pinch of nutmeg.

COCO SOUP

4 cocos
1 lb. soup meat
2 qrts. water

2 slices of bacon
1 tablespoon butter

Chop up cocos and place in a pot with water and soup meat and bacon. Boil until cos are soft and meat is cooked.

Remove meat, put cocos and liquid through a blender or sieve.

Season to taste. Add the meat and a dab of margarine. Reheat to serve.

COCKEREL SOUP

4 lb. cockerel (a young cock)
2 qrts. water
2 sliced carrots

2 sliced potatoes
* onion, thyme, salt and a hot pepper

Boil the cockerel in water. When tender, strain and skim. Add vegetables, seasonings, and strips of the meat to the liquid.

Boil until vegetables are tender. Water may be added if it has boiled away.

Remove the hot pepper without breaking it in the cooking liquid.

COLD THICK CUCUMBER SOUP

½ cup diced cucumber
¾ cup diced cooked chicken
1 cup diced and cooked lobster meat
¼ cup chopped onion

1 cup milk
2 tablespoons sour cream
* salt, pepper, parsley

Mix the milk into the sour cream and thin down. Add all other ingredients. Chill for 2 hours before serving.

BEET SOUP

8 large cooked and peeled beets
1 lb. soup meat cut into cubes
3 diced tomatoes
2 qrts. water

1 cup shredded cabbage
* salt, pepper
* sour cream

Combine meat, tomatoes and water in a saucepan. Bring to a boil. Skim and cook for about an hour.

Add the cabbage, salt, and pepper. Cook for 30 minutes.

Grate the beetroots and add to the soup with salt and pepper. Cook for 15 minutes.

Serve very hot, with a spoonful of sour cream and a few pieces of the meat in each soup bowl.

COW HEEL SOUP

1 pr. cow heels
6 cups water
1 chopped onion
1 diced chocho
1 diced carrot

1 chopped coco
1 hot pepper
2 teaspoons salt
* squeeze of lime juice
* parsley

Wash cow heels in lime juice. Cut up and boil in salted water. Skim frequently. Cook 2–3 hours over low heat.

Add vegetables and seasonings. Boil until vegetables are tender. Serve with chopped parsley.

FISH CHOWDER

2 lbs. of any type of white fish meat
1 qrt. water
1 minced onion
2 diced carrots

1 diced potato
2 diced tomatoes
* salt and pepper to taste
* sherry, optional

Boil fish in water until tender. Remove all bones and strain the liquid. Stir diced vege tables into fish stock with seasonings. When cooked add some flaked fish meat and sher to taste.

JAMAICA FISH TEA

3 lbs. of fish cut into pieces
6 cups water
2 chopped onions
2 chopped tomatoes

1 hot pepper
1 tsp. thyme
* squeeze of lime juice

Place all ingredients in a pot with water. Bring to a boil and simmer gently for abc an hour.
Strain off liquid and serve with chopped parsley.

GOAT HEAD SOUP (surya)— India

1 goat head
1 lb. pumpkin
1 lb. carrots
1 chocho
6 green bananas
1 lb. yellow yam

12 small dumplings
1 chopped onion
* herbs, salt, pepper and a small
  piece of crushed ginger root
3 qrts. water

Prepare and clean goat's head. Put to boil in a large soup pot with water. Skim. Wh meat is tender, remove bones and put flesh back into liquid. Keep boiling.
Prepare and add the vegetables, seasoning and peppers. Soup must be of thick cons tency. Serves 6.

GUNGU OR COW PEA SOUP

1 pint of peas (soaked overnight)
2 qrts. water
1 lb. soup meat

1 sliced coco
1 chopped onion
* thyme, salt, pepper

Boil peas with soup meat in water until tender. Remove the meat and put peas throu a colander, rub out and discard skin.
Place liquid on stove with seasonings and coco. Add more water if necessary.
When coco is cooked and dissolved, the soup is ready. Bits of the boiled meat can added.

PAW PAW (PAPAYA) SOUP – Nigeria

tablespoons butter
sliced onion
paw paw peeled, seeded and sliced –
use a fruit which is past the green
stage but not yet ripe

3 cups water
* a sprig of parsley
* salt, pepper and a dash of nutmeg
3 cups milk
1 tablespoon cornstarch

Melt butter and fry onions. Add the paw paw, water, parsley, salt and pepper. Cover d boil over a low heat for about one hour, or until paw paw is tender enough to force rough a sieve.

Return to saucepan and add nutmeg. Mix cornstarch into milk until smooth, and add the paw paw mixture. Stir, constantly.

Cook for 10 minutes more over low heat, but do not allow to boil.

PEPPER POT

lbs. of chopped callaloo or spinach
qrts. water
lb. soup meat
slices bacon or a pig's tail
lb. pre-cooked shrimp

1 doz. okras sliced
1 minced onion
1 diced coco
* salt, pepper, herbs, hot pepper to taste

Place meat and bacon in a soup pot with water. Boil until meat is tender.

Add callaloo,okras, coco and seasonings. Simmer until soup has thickened.

Remove hot pepper and meat (or may be left in if desired). Small flour dumplings ptional) and the shrimps are added. Simmer for 15 minutes longer.

PUMPKIN SOUP

lbs. pumpkin
qrts. water
lb. soup meat
a small piece of salt pork

3 pieces chopped escallion
1 chopped coco
* thyme, salt, hot pepper

Place meat and salt pork in water and boil until meat is tender. Remove the meats.

Add peeled diced pumpkin, seasonings and chopped coco. Boil until vegetables are dis-lved.

Taste for seasoning. Press through a colander and heat to serve.

SEA WEED SOUP (Irish Moss)

cups chicken broth
chopped onion
beaten egg

1 cup washed sea weed
* salt and pepper

Mix chicken broth, onion, sea weed and seasonings. Bring to a boil and simmer for out 20 minutes.

Remove the sea weed and add the beaten egg to the broth when it is cool. Reheat to ve, but do not boil.

RED PEA SOUP

1 pint of red peas (soak overnight)	1 sliced coco
2 qrts. water	1 minced onion
1 lb. soup meat	* salt, thyme, hot pepper to taste
¼ lb. of pig's tail	

Place peas and meats in water. Boil until peas are almost tender. Add coco and seasonings. When peas and coco are cooked, remove the meats.

Soup may be served with whole peas, or, put through a colander and discard skin. Small dumplings are usually added to this soup.

TRIPE SOUP

4 lbs. tripe	2 diced potatoes
½ cup vinegar	2 cups diced chochos
1 pair pig's trotters	* salt and pepper
2 chopped onions	4 qrts. water

Soak tripe and trotters in vinegar with water to cover for 2 hours. Drain and rinse. Place tripe, trotters and 4 qrts. of water into a pot. Bring to a boil and skim. Cook over a low heat for about 3 hours.

Strain off the liquid. Cut tripe into small pieces and set aside. Discard trotters. Using about 6 cups of the liquid, add seasonings and vegetables. Cook for about ½ hour.

Add the tripe and simmer for a further ten minutes. Correct seasoning. This is a thick soup.

CLEAR TURTLE SOUP

3 lbs. of turtle meat	* salt – thyme – 6 pimento grains
3 qrts. of water	* lime peel – a pinch of sage
3 diced carrots	* sherry to taste
2 diced onions	

Set all ingredients except lime peel and sage to boil for about 3 hours. One hour before straining, add a piece of lime peel, and some sage. Strain through a fine sieve.

Add some sherry and pieces of the turtle meat when serving.

THICK TURTLE SOUP

This is prepared in the same way as Clear Turtle Soup, except that it is thickened with 1 oz. of cornflour mixed with a little liquid for every qrt. of the soup.

Fish & Shellfish

STUFFED CALAPEEVA
(found in Jamaican rivers)

calapeeva	2 sliced onions
cup breadcrumbs	1 tablespoon rum
parsley, salt, pepper to taste	1 tablespoon oil
dessertspoon butter	

Wash and clean fish with lime juice. Make a stuffing of breadcrumbs, parsley, salt and pepper, moistened with a little melted butter.

Stuff the fish and place on a bed of sliced onions, which have been slightly sauteed in hot oil. Add 1 tablespoon rum and cover with some breadcrumbs. Bake in a moderate oven until fish are tender.

STAMP AND GO (CODFISH FRITTERS)

lb. salted codfish	1 minced onion
lime juice	1 diced tomato
lb. flour	¼ teaspoon hot pepper sauce
water	

Wash codfish with lime juice, dry, and mince with onions and tomatoes. Add the flour and hot sauce with a little water to make a batter.

Heat some oil in a skillet. Drop the mixture by spoonfuls into the skillet and press down so that fritters are quite thin.

Fry on both sides until golden brown and crisp. Drain on paper towel and serve warm.

BANANA KING FISH WITH MUSTARD SAUCE

4 king fish steaks
2 ripe bananas
4 slices Cheddar cheese

* salt
* pepper
* butter

Season the fish steaks with salt and pepper. Fry gently in butter.

Place the steaks in a heat-proof dish. Cover each steak with slices of ripe banana and top with a slice of cheddar cheese. Broil until the cheese is melted and the banana heated through. Serve with mustard sauce.

Mustard Sauce

4 tablespoons mayonnaise
4 tablespoons vinegar
4 tablespoons salad oil

1 teaspoon lime juice
3 teaspoons dry mustard
* salt and pepper to taste

Mix all ingredients until smooth.

CODFISH BALLS

1 lb. codfish
1 lb. fresh pumpkin
1 tablespoon butter, softened
2 eggs

* black pepper
* salt
2 cups fresh breadcrumbs
* oil

Soak fish overnight. Discard water and cover with cold water. Bring to a boil and cook until tender. Skin, bone and flake finely.

Cook the pumpkin until tender. Mash thoroughly then beat in the softened butter, 2 lightly beaten eggs and pepper. Add salt to taste. The mixture should be firm enough to hold its shape. If not, beat in breadcrumbs as needed.

Shape the mixture into balls, dipping each in the breadcrumbs. Fry for about 3 to 4 minutes, turning regularly. When golden brown, drain on paper towels. Serve warm. A tomato sauce goes well with this dish.

BAKED BLACK CRABS

6 Black Crabs, boiled
1 oz. butter, softened
½ teaspoon black pepper
1 tablespoon chopped onion
1 country pepper, finely chopped

1 teaspoon vinegar
* salt
* breadcrumbs
* butter

Clean the crabs and pick out all the meat, including the claws and smaller bones. Save four shells.

Mix the crab meat with the butter, onion, pepper, salt and vinegar. The mixture should be moist but not soggy.

Wash the shells well and wipe with a little oil. Fill each with the crab mixture, top with the breadcrumbs and dot with butter. Bake in a hot oven until the crumbs are brown.

BAHAMIAN CONCH FRITTERS

1 lb. raw minced conch meat
1 minced onion
4 ozs. flour
1 egg

* salt, pepper
2 tablespoons dry breadcrumbs
* milk and fat as needed

Mix conch meat, onion, flour, egg and seasoning together and moisten with a little milk. Shape into flat fritters. Dip in breadcrumbs and fry quickly in hot oil.

CODFISH TWICE LAID

1 lb. salt fish
1 lb. potatoes, boiled & sliced
1 sliced onion

2 tablespoons margarine or butter
* breadcrumbs
* pepper to taste

Soak fish overnight. Discard water and cover with cold water. Bring to a boil and cook until tender. Skin, bone and flake.

Fry onion lightly and add to the fish. In a casserole place alternate layers of potatoes with fish-onion mixture. Dot layers with butter and cover with breadcrumbs before baking until golden brown in a moderate oven.

SALTFISH AND ACKEE

1 lb. codfish
12–14 ackees
2 ozs. fried bacon
4 ozs. margarine

2 tablespoons margarine or butter
* breadcrumbs
* pepper to taste

Soak fish overnight and discard the water. Cover with cold water and boil until tender. Skin, bone and flake, and set aside.

Prepare ackees and boil quickly. In a separate pan, melt margarine, stir in onions tomatoes and pepper. Simmer a few minutes, then add the fish and ackees. Heat through to serve.

CRAB FRITTERS

½ lb. cooked crab meat (use local black crabs)
2 tablespoons oil
1 tablespoon chopped onion

3 eggs
1 tablespoon minced parsley
* breadcrumbs, salt, pepper to taste

Add onion, seasoning and beaten egg to crab meat. Add enough breadcrumbs to bind mixture. Shape into fritters and fry lightly.

13

ESCOVEITCH OF FISH (GROUPER)

* small fish or slices of king fish
* oil
1 cup vinegar
2 sliced onions

2 tablespoons water
1 chopped hot pepper
* a pimento leaf and a pinch of salt

Fry fish in hot oil and set aside. Mix remaining ingredients together and bring to a boil Simmer 20 minutes.

Lay fish in a shallow dish. Cover with hot vinegar sauce and marinate for about 1½ hours before serving.

(In Mexico the fish is not cooked, it is marinated and eaten raw.)

FISH KEDGEREE

1 cup cooked rice
* curry powder
* mushrooms, optional
* lime rind

1 cup cooked fish, tuna, salmon
  or codfish
* salt
3 hard-boiled eggs

Toss together cooked rice and flaked, cooked fish. Add a pinch of curry powder an some chopped mushrooms if available, a pinch of salt and a sprinkle of lime rind.

Pack into a mould and bake for 30 minutes. Serve with chopped hard boiled eggs

---

JAMAICA FISH PIE

2 cups cooked flaked fish
1 cup white sauce (see page 43)
1 cup cooked peeled shrimps
* salt, pepper, chopped parsley

1 cup cooked, mashed potatoes
1 cup flour
* pinch of salt
1 beaten egg

Mix together fish, white sauce, shrimp, seasonings and parsley and place in a deep pi dish.

Mix remaining ingredients to form a dough. Roll out on a floured board and cut t cover pie.

Place dough over fish mixture and prick top with a fork. Bake in a moderate ove about 30 minutes or till crust is brown.

BAKED GRUNTS

6 grunts
* juice of 2 limes
* water, hot pepper, salt

3 tablespoons butter
* avocado slices

Clean grunts, place in a greased dish and add lime juice and water to cover. Add salt and pieces of hot pepper.

Cover and bake in a 350° oven for about 20 minutes. Spread melted butter over the and serve with avocado slices.

KING FISH IN COCONUT CREAM

lbs. fish steaks
ozs. butter or margarine
cup coconut cream

* salt, pepper
* lime slices

Heat butter and fry steaks until brown on both sides.
To make coconut cream, grate a coconut, add water, squeeze and strain out cream.
Discard pulp.
Add to fish steaks with salt and pepper.
Simmer for about 3 minutes. Garnish with lime slices.

KING FISH FILLETS

fillets of king fish
glass white wine
cup cooked and peeled shrimps
cup white sauce
egg

* a pinch of salt and pepper
* a squeeze of lime juice
2 tablespoons tomato sauce
1 cup breadcrumbs
2-3 tablespoons margarine or oil

Soak fillets in white wine, salt, pepper, and lime juice for 1 hour. Pat dry.
Make 1 cup of white sauce and add the cooked shrimps. When this is cool, spoon some
of the mixture onto each fish and roll up.
Dip in breadcrumbs, then into beaten egg and again in crumbs. Fry in hot oil. Serve
with tomato sauce.

LOBSTER CREOLE

lbs. cooked and shredded lobster
meat
chopped onions
chopped sweet peppers

3 diced tomatoes
2 tablespoons rum or sherry
4 tablespoons oil
* salt, pepper, to taste

Fry onion and peppers until tender. Stir in salt and pepper. Add tomatoes and simmer
gently. Add lobster meat with rum or sherry.
Continue to simmer gently for about 10 minutes. Serve with plain boiled rice.

MACKEREL ALOHA

tin drained mackerel
cup diced pineapple
tablespoons chopped peanuts

¼ cup mayonnaise
1 tablespoon lime juice

Break up mackerel. Combine with remaining ingredients and toss.
Serve in shells or lettuce cups.
Sardines can also be served in this manner.

OCTOPUS (called by local fishermen "Sea Puss")

1 small octopus
3 tablespoons butter

* salted water to cover

Cut octopus into small pieces and place in a pot of salted water. Bring to a boil and cook until octopus is tender. Drain, dry and fry in butter. Serve with one of the following sauces.

PIQUANT SAUCE

1 tablespoon oil
2 tablespoons vinegar

½ chopped onion
* pinch salt and pepper

Mix all ingredients together.

CHEESE SAUCE

6 tablespoons flour
6 tablespoons margarine
2 cups milk

1 cup grated cheese
* salt to taste

Melt margarine and blend in flour and milk. Stir all the time until thick. Add cheese and salt. Heat until cheese is melted.

SHRIMP WITH PINEAPPLE

24 large shrimp, cleaned, peeled and
    cooked
1 tablespoon cornflour
½ pint pineapple juice
2 tablespoons soya sauce

1 tablespoon honey
1 tablespoon vinegar
¼ teaspoon ginger powder
1 small tin of pineapple chunks

Blend cornflour with a little of the pineapple juice. Combine with remaining juice, soya sauce, honey, vinegar and ginger. Cook over a low heat, stirring until thickened.
Thread shrimps and pineapple chunks alternately on to skewers and dip into sauce. Grill until slightly golden in colour.

BAKED SPICY SNOOK
(found in Jamaican rivers)

lbs. snook (prepared)
tablespoon salt
teaspoon pepper
teaspoon nutmeg

1 tablespoon onion
½ cup melted butter
¼ cup soya sauce
2 tablespoons lime juice

Mix salt, pepper, nutmeg, onion and rub into the fish, inside and outside.
Wrap in foil and bake about 20 minutes in a moderate oven.
Whilst fish is baking combine butter, lime juice and soya sauce. At the end of 20 min-
es pour this sauce over the fish.
Cover and bake 20 minutes longer.

SOLOMON GUNDY

lb. pickled herring
lb. pickled shad
3 cup vinegar
tablespoon oil

1 tablespoon chopped onion
* a few pimento grains
* a few drops of hot pepper sauce

Soak the fish for 3 hours in water to cover. Pour off the water and scald the fish with
iling water. Remove the skin, let cool, and shred flesh.
Boil vinegar with onion and pimento grains. Add oil and pour over fish.
Pack into jars, cover and keep in the refrigerator.

RED STRIPE BATTER FOR FISH

cup cornstarch
cup flour
cup beer (Red Stripe)

2 egg whites
¼ cup margarine or oil
* salt to taste

Any type of fish may be used.
Mix cornstarch and flour and salt. Add beer and beat until smooth. Beat egg whites
d fold into batter.
Dip slices of fish or whole small fish into this batter and fry in bubbling fat.

17

CHICKEN BAHAMAS

1 3 lb. chicken
2 cups cooked rice or spaghetti
3 ozs. cashew nuts

* hot pepper sauce to taste
* salt
2 chopped onions

Boil a chicken in the usual way. Reserve stock. Cut chicken into pieces and arrange on bed of rice, or spaghetti. Prepare a sauce by pounding cashew nuts with some hot peppe sauce and a pinch of salt.

Fry two onoins and add to nut mixture, with some of the chicken stock. Pour ov the chicken.

DRUNK CHICKEN

2 lbs. chicken cut in pieces
2 qrts. water

1 teaspoon salt
* sherry or rum or white wine

Heat to boiling 2 qrts. of water, salt and chicken; Cover and simmer for about 15 min-utes.

Place chicken in a bowl or jar and cover completely with liquor. Keep refrigerated for 1 week. Serve cold.

CHICKEN WITH LIME AND OLIVES

2½ lbs. chicken
¼ cup oil
1½ cups minced onions
½ teaspoon powdered ginger

1½ cups water
1 tablespoon lime juice
2 doz. small pitted olives
* salt, pepper

Cut chicken into pieces and brown on all sides in oil. Remove chicken and fry onions.
Stir in ginger, salt and pepper and simmer 2 minutes. Add water, lime juice and chicken pieces. Simmer for 30 minutes. Add olives a few minutes before serving.

TROPICAL CHICKEN

young coconuts
small chicken
cups chicken broth
cup rice
cup chopped pineapple

1 diced onion
½ cup corn kernels
3 tablespoons curry powder
* salt, pepper

Slice off top of coconuts and take a thin slice off the bottoms also, so that the coco-
it will stand upright. Pour off water and reserve.

Steam chicken in coconut water. When tender, remove, cool and shred the meat.
Steam rice in 2 cups of broth (adding water if needed). Mix in pineapple, onions, corn
d curry powder. Correct seasoning.

Stuff coconuts with this mixture, placing alternate layers with the shredded chicken.
place tops on coconut and sit in a shallow pan of water. Bake in a moderate oven for
e hour. If water in pan evaporates add more.

A DIFFERENT STUFFING
FOR ROASTED CHICKEN

cup cooked rice
cup raisins
cup finely chopped onions
chopped parsley

* diced cooked chicken liver
2 ozs. butter
1 egg

Mash the chicken livers and mix all ingredients together, working the butter well into
xture. Add the beaten egg last to bind.

GUINEA HEN AFRICAN STYLE

lb. butter or margarine
small guinea hens cut into pieces
minced onion
tablespoon flour
cup water

3 chopped tomatoes
3 sweet potatoes, cubed
5 firm ripe plantains, sliced
* salt, pepper

Melt all but 3 tablespoons butter in a large pot or casserole. Add the guinea hen pieces,
ons, some salt and pepper and saute in some of the butter. Sprinkle with flour and add
ter and tomatoes.

Cook over low heat for 25 minutes. Add sweet potato cubes and cook until tender.
rrect seasoning.

Melt remaining butter and fry plantain slices. Skim all fat from gravy and serve plan-
n slices separately.

BRAISED GUINEA HEN

1 prepared guinea hen
* fat
1 lump of butter
1 lb. carrots

1 clove garlic
1 sliced onion
* parsley, thyme, salt, pepper to taste

Put butter inside guinea hen and brown in sizzling fat.

Clean and slice carrots lengthwise and add to pan with garlic, onion and herbs. Cov and cook about an hour depending on the age of the bird. Wine may be added to t sauce.

GUINEA FOWL STEW

1 guinea fowl
4 onions
2 tomatoes
2 hard boiled eggs
2 cups crushed peanuts

1 cup water
2 cloves garlic
½ teaspoon salt
* oil
* boiled white rice

Put peanuts into 1 cup water and boil for 12 minutes until the peanut oil shows on t side of the pot.

Cut up guinea fowl and saute in oil. Add diced tomatoes, onions and garlic. Finall add all the peanuts and seasoning. Mix well and fry for 5 minutes.

Empty into a pot adding more water if needed and stew until flesh is tender.

When cooked, float halved hard boiled eggs on the top and serve with boiled white ric

---

PIGEONS WITH CABBAGE

2 pigeons
1 small cabbage
1 onion
2 pieces bacon
½ cup water

* juice of 1 lime
½ cup raisins
* a pinch of salt
* sugar and pepper to taste

Cut the birds in half down the backbone. Melt fat from bacon and fry the birds in th Remove birds.

Slice onion and saute in the same pan. Add sugar and raisins. Shred cabbage and add the pan. Stir to coat.

Heat water and lime juice and add to pan with a sprinkle of salt.

Place the pieces of pigeons on top of the cabbage. Cover and simmer for about 1 hou Correct seasoning.

PIGEON PIE

3 pigeons cut into pieces
* salt and pepper
3 tablespoons oil

* diced ham
2 cups chicken broth

Season pigeons with salt and pepper and fry in oil. Add diced ham and stock. Place in a deep pie dish and cover with crust. Bake in 350° oven 30 minutes or till crust is lightly browned.

PIE CRUST

1 cup flour
4 ozs. butter, margarine or shortening

2-3 tablespoons cold water
* pinch of salt

Sift together flour and salt. Mix fat into flour by using 2 knives and "cutting" in the fat till it is pea-sized and coated with flour. Sprinkle water over flour using a minimum amount to moisten mixture. Shape mixture into a mound and roll out. Cut to fit dish.

PIGEONS WITH PINEAPPLE

½ of a ripe pineapple
4 squabs (young pigeons)
¼ cup butter
¼ cup paté

4 tablespoons brandy or rum if preferred
* salt, pepper to taste
½ cup pineapple juice

Peel, slice and dice pineapple. Wash and dry squabs. Into each body cavity put 1 tablespoon pate and a piece of pineapple. Close cavity and rub squabs with salt and pepper.
Melt ½ of the butter in a heavy casserole and brown the squabs. Do not prick the skins.
Flame with 1 tablespoon brandy or rum (heat, ignite and pour over squabs). Pour in the remaining butter, and roast squabs in 350° oven uncovered, basting often, for about 45 minutes.
While squabs are roasting, poach slices of pineapple in the rest of liquor for 10 minutes. Arrange slices on the squabs to serve.

BALDPATE SPATCHCOCK

3 baldpate doves
2 tablespoons melted butter
1 teaspoon salt

1 teaspoon pepper
* juice of a lime
* fat for basting

Prepare doves, wash with lime juice and season. Split through the backbone and flatten the birds. Wipe dry.
Bake in hot oven basting frequently for about 15 minutes.
Remove from the oven, place under a grill, dribble melted butter over the birds and grill on both sides.

WHITE WING OR ANY OTHER
DOVE WITH CREAM

4 doves
4 slices bacon
4 tablespoons butter

¼ pint cream (or evaporated milk)
*   a few black olives
*   salt and pepper to taste

Cover the breast of each bird with a slice of bacon and season. Place 1 tablespoon butter inside each bird.

Roast in a hot 400-450° oven for 30 minutes. Remove birds, drain off surplus fat and add cream to the pan.

Simmer slowly and season to taste. Add olives, and pour over the birds.

BRAISED DUCKLING

1 3½–4 lb. duckling
4 ozs. butter
2 onions
2 carrots
¼ cup brandy or wine

1 cup chicken stock
½ lb. young sliced turnips
2 ozs. butter
* salt, pepper to taste

Brown duck on all sides in a casserole. Put in the onions and sliced carrots, browning them also.

Pour in the liquor and all the stock with salt and pepper. Place in a moderate oven 350° and baste frequently.

When duck is ready, keep it warm. Strain the liquid, remove vegetables and reduce the sauce.

Serve with the young turnips which have been cooked whilst duck was braising. Blanch the turnips first, then saute in butter.

SALMI OF DUCK

1 duck
2 ozs. butter
1 oz. flour
1 onion, chopped

1½ pints chicken stock (chicken cubes
    melted in water)
* salt, pepper
* brandy or wine

Roast duck, cook till slightly underdone. Cut into neat joints.

Melt 1 oz. butter and fry onion. Add stock, simmer for 1 hour and strain. Melt remaining butter, stir in flour and add the stock. Season and simmer 15 minutes.

Add the pieces of duck and cook 20 minutes longer. Brandy or wine is usually added to taste.

DUCK AND PINEAPPLE

4lb. duck
tin pineapple slices
tablespoons oil
tablespoons soya sauce

1 tablespoon rum
½ cup water
2 tablespoons brown sugar
* a pinch of salt

Clean and roast the duck. Cool, remove bones and slice. Drain pineapple slices and dice.
Place duck and pineapple in alternate layers in a casserole. Add the pineapple juice
ixed with oil, soya sauce, rum, water, sugar and salt.
Bake in moderate oven for 1 hour. Serve with rice and green salad.

TEAL WITH ORANGE SAUCE

teal (wild duck)
salt and pepper

* oil

Prepare and season birds. Roast till done, in a moderate oven, basting with cooking
ts and adding a little oil if necessary.

AUCE

juice of 2 oranges
2 cloves
dessertspoon cornstarch

1 tablespoon rum
* orange segments

Mix juice with cloves and thicken with cornstarch moistened first in some of the juice.
dd rum and orange juice to liquid and boil very slowly to thicken in a double boiler.
rve over teal.

BEEF CURRY WITH GREEN BANANAS

3 peeled green bananas cut in ¼" slices
1½ lbs. stewing beef ·
3 tablespoons oil
2 tablespoons curry powder
2 onions

1½ tablespoons flour
½ cup tomato ketchup
½ teaspoon salt
½ cup rum

Boil bananas in salted water for 20 minutes. Drain and reserve.

Cut beef into cubes and brown in oil. Transfer to a saucepan.

Add sliced onions. Stir in flour, salt and tomato ketchup and cook for 5 min
Cover with curry powder mixed in some water. Stir and simmer for 1½ hrs. Add run
green banana slices. Heat through.

BEEF AND MANGO IN BEER

12 ozs. minced beef
1 cup Red Stripe Beer
1 cup water
½ cup mango chutney

* pinch of salt and onion powder
1 dessertspoon soya sauce
½ cup rice
1 cup green peas

Combine first six ingredients in a casserole and bake in oven for 1 hour at 3
Add rice and cook for ½ hour. Just before serving add the peas.

SALTED BEEF AND
BANANA CASSEROLE

¼ lb. diced, cooked, salted beef
2 eggs
1 cup grated cheese

½ cup milk
1 cup diced ripe bananas
* salt, pepper, marjoram

Beat eggs, stir in cheese, beef, milk, pepper, marjoram and bananas. Use very little
if any. Turn into a casserole and bake for about 40 minutes in a 350° oven.

DUMPERPUMPKIN

1 small pumpkin   ½ cup seeded prunes
2 cups prepared sweet and sour beef

Wash pumpkin and place in a large pot. Cover with water and bring to a boil. When cooked, but not soft, remove, cut off the top and scoop out seeds and core.

Fill with sweet and sour beef mix and prunes. Refit top. Place pumpkin in a baking dish with water and bake for 30-40 minutes in a moderate oven — add more water if necessary.

SWEET AND SOUR BEEF FILLING

2 lbs. steak, cubed   1 teaspoon soya sauce
* fat or oil   1 teaspoon tomato ketchup
1 tablespoon sugar   * pinch of salt and ginger powder
1 cup water   1 dessertspoon cornstarch
3 tablespoons vinegar

Fry steak in oil and cook through. In a separate pot, bring next six ingredients to a boil and thicken with a little cornstarch blended in some water.

Pour over the cubed steak. Simmer for about ½ hour.

Fill pumpkin cavity and transfer to oven for 30 mins.

RUMP STEAK CASSEROLE

2 lbs. steak   * salt, pepper, nutmeg and ginger
¼ lb. margarine   to taste
1 dessertspoon sugar   1 teaspoon marjoram
1 cup vinegar   * chopped tomatoes, optional
1 cup beef stock (tin of beef bouillon or consomme)

Cut steaks into cubes and marinate for 2 hours in sugar, vinegar, seasoning and herbs. Melt margarine and brown beef cubes. Moisten with some of the marinade.

Place meat in a casserole with 1 cup of beef stock. Cover and bake in a 350° oven until tender.

Skim off fat and add a few chopped tomatoes if desired.

POOR MAN'S FILLET

3 lbs. rib eye steak
2 tablespoons butter

* salt, pepper, garlic powder to taste
* bread slices

Cut the steak allowing one slice per person. Rub with salt, pepper and garlic. Bro▪ steak slices in hot butter. Fry slices of bread in butter.

Slip a slice of steak onto each slice of bread and serve with sauce from rry pan. Tal▪ about 3 minutes to prepare.

CURRIED GOAT OR RABBIT

1 lb. goat or rabbit
2 tablespoons curry powder
2 sliced onions
2 cups hot water

1 tablespoon lime juice
1 tablespoon butter
* salt, oil

Cut meat into bite-size pieces, season with curry powder and salt and set aside f▪ about one hour. Brown in hot oil.

Add 2 cups of hot water and onions. Cook slowly until tender, stirring to prevent bu▪ ing. Add more curry powder if needed, butter and lime juice. Cook for about 20 minu▪ longer.

Serve with plain boiled rice and side dishes of nuts, grated coconut, mango chutne▪ sliced onions soaked in hot sauce and slices of fried ripe plantain.

BONED STUFFED LEG OF KID

1 boned leg of goat kid
1 cup breadcrumbs
* milk

1 egg yolk
* chopped parsley
* salt and pepper

Season mea▪ with salt and pepper. Moisten breadcrumbs with milk and press dr▪ Add egg yolk, chopped parsley, salt and pepper to make a stuffing for meat.

Fill, roll, and tie meat and bake for 1½ hours in a 350° oven. Serve with baby carro▪ and small boiled onions.

MUTTON STEW (In Jamaica goat meat is often referred to as mutton)

3 lbs. goat meat
1 teaspoon hot sauce
1 cup chopped onions
* oil, salt, flour
1 cup sliced carrots

1 cup chopped tomatoes
1 cup sliced potatoes
4 cups hot water
* some small flour dumplings

Dredge cubed meat with flour and salt and brown in hot oil. Add water and simme▪ until meat is tender.

Add sauce, onions, and vegetables. Cook until vegetables are ready. This proces▪ should take about 2 hours.

When all is ready add the dumplings which will cook very quickly. Add more liquid ▪ necessary.

LIVER WITH SWEET PEPPERS

lb. liver sliced thin
sweet peppers
teaspoon lime juice

1 tablespoon rum
½ cup oil
* salt, pepper, a little flour

Prepare sweet peppers by coring and removing seeds. Wash and cut into strips.
Season liver with salt, pepper and lime juice. Dust with flour and saute quickly in hot
il.
Pour the rum over liver. Add the slices of pepper and cook gently for 15-20 minutes.

PORK CHOPS WITH GINGER ALE

chops
fat, salt, pepper

* parsley
* ginger ale

Brown chops lightly in fat. Add seasoning. Place in individual squares of foil. Sprinkle
berally with ginger ale. Fold squares tightly. Place in a baking dish and bake in a 350°
ven for about 1½ hours.

MARINATED PORK CHOPS

chops
salt, pepper

* lime juice
* garlic powder

Sprinkle the chops with seasonings and lime juice and marinate for 2 hours. Grill the
hops and serve with a green salad. Instead of a dressing pour the juices from the grilling
an.

PORK CHOPS WITH PINEAPPLE

chops
cup pineapple chunks
prunes or 1 cup raisins
teaspoon grated lime peel
sprinkle of sugar and salt
breadcrumbs

* a lump of butter
2 cups shredded cabbage
* salt
¼ cup vinegar
1 tablespoon water

Brown chops and sprinkle with salt. In a casserole, place the chops in layers with
he pineapple, prunes, peel and sugar.
Cover with breadcrumbs and dot with butter. Bake in a slow oven 300° for 1½ hours.
Serve with shredded cabbage which has been sprinkled with salt and boiled in vinegar
nd water. When tender, strain and serve hot.

27

JERKED PORK SNACKS

1   3–4 lbs. boned leg of pork
    (cut into bite size pieces)
1   cup vinegar   *   crushed pimento leaves
*   chopped hot pepper   *   pimento grains, salt
*   chopped onion and garlic

Marinate the pieces of pork in the marinade for 4 days turning frequently. Keep
covered in refrigerator.

Take out and wipe dry. Cook pork on a grid over burning coals to get a smokey
flavour; however, it can also be baked crisp on a baking sheet in the oven.

RABBIT FRICASSEE

1   rabbit cut into pieces   2   slices bacon
2   tablespoons vinegar   1   cup chicken broth
*   oil or fat   2   tablespoons raisins
*   salt and pepper   1   dessertspoon grated chocolate
2   sliced onions   1   teaspoon sugar

Wash rabbit in vinegar. Pat dry and saute in fat with sliced onions, bacon and seasoning.
Add broth and simmer slowly until rabbit is tender.

Add the sugar, chocolate and raisins to finish cooking. Do not be afraid of the chocolate, it gives a surprisingly pleasant flavour to this dish.

BRAWN (made also with Rabbit
using the whole animal)

1   pig's head   *   lime to taste
*   water, pimento leaves   *   salt to taste
*   few cloves

Scrape and clean the head and wash with lime juice. Cover with water, pimento leaves,
salt and cloves. Boil until tender.

Cut into chunks discarding the bones. Add lime juice to the liquid and pour over the
brawn in a casserole. Place in the refrigerator to congeal.

ROASTED RABBIT

rabbit (skin and clean)
sage
tablespoon butter
cup milk

* salt, pepper
1 cup breadcrumbs
* bacon drippings

Stuff rabbit with breadcrumbs mixed with the given ingredients. Sew up cavity. Rub over with bacon dripping. Roast 1–1½ hrs. in a 350° oven.

SOUSE (From Barbados)

pig's head
pig's tongue
pig's trotters
limes
tablespoon salt

¼ pint beef stock
1 sliced onion
* hot peppers to taste
* juice from 2 limes

Scald and scrape meats and wash with lime juice. Tie all meats into a cloth with a ˈinkle of salt. Place in a pot and cover with cold water. Boil up and simmer for about 2 ˈurs.
Cool in the liquid. Remove meat, skin and slice the tongue. Cut up the trotters and ˈe the meat from head. Place in a deep casserole.
Bring remaining ingredients to a boil and pour over meats.
Cover and reheat to serve. Can be used hot or chilled.

TRIPE WINDSOR

lbs. tripe
qrt. water
onions
carrots
cup stock
salt, thyme, parsley to taste

1 chopped onion
4 chopped tomatoes
1 tablespoon brandy
2 ozs. margarine
* grated nutmeg
* salt and pepper

Wash tripe with lime juice and put into a stew pot with the water. Simmer for 2 hours. Add vegetables, herbs and salt and simmer until tripe is tender and the vegetables ɔked. Remove tripe from the stock and cut into small pieces.
Mix tripe and vegetables with remaining ingredients in a covered casserole. Bake in a ˈderate oven for 35 minutes.

BEANS IN SOUR CREAM SAUCE

1 lb. green beans (string beans)   * salt
2 tablespoons butter

    Boil beans uncovered, strain, melt butter, add beans and toss. Season with sal
pepper. Top with this sauce.

SAUCE

1 cup sour cream   * a few drops of lime juice,
¼ cup milk   * a pinch of garlic powder

    Mix ingredients together and pour over beans.

BROAD BEAN CUTLETS

1 lb. broad beans (or sugar beans)   1 teaspoon chopped parsley
1 oz. margarine   6 ozs. crushed potatoes
2 eggs   * bread crumbs
1 teaspoon minced onion   * salt and pepper to taste

    Cook beans in boiling water with salt and onions. Puree by rubbing through a
    Add melted margarine, crushed potatoes, seasoning, and enough of the beaten e
bind into a paste. Add enough bread crumbs to shape into cutlets and coat with eg
more bread crumbs. Fry in deep hot fat. Drain and serve warm.

STUFFED BREADFRUIT

medium size breadfruit
tablespoon butter
cup milk

1 small chopped onion
* a pinch of salt

Stuffed breadfruit is first roasted for an hour in the skin — roasted over charcoal is of course the best way, but it can be done over a gas burner.

When cooked, cut a circle in the top, scoop out heart and discard, then scoop out the flesh.

Crush this, cream with milk and butter and season with a little salt and onion. To this may be added minced beef, codfish and ackee, or left over stew etc.

Pack into the cavity, wrap with foil and put into the oven to warm through before serving.

BAKED CABBAGE

cups shredded cabbage
cups breadcrumbs
cup grated cheese
eggs

1 teaspoon salt
1 teaspoon prepared mustard
2 cups milk
1/8 teaspoon pepper

Cover cabbage with water, bring to a boil and drain. In a shallow 2 qrt. dish, arrange cabbage, breadcrumbs and cheese in layers.

Beat eggs with salt, pepper and mustard. Add milk and pour over the cabbage. Let stand for 15 minutes. Bake for 45 minutes in a 350° oven.

FRUITED CABBAGE

½ lbs. shredded cabbage
ozs. raisins
diced onions

1 cup water
1 cup diced pineapple
* juice of 1 lime

Mix cabbage with fruit and onions. Add 1 cup water, lime juice and a pinch of salt. Cook for about 40 minutes or until liquid has evaporated.

CALLALOO BAKE

bunch callaloo cooked and diced
diced onion
slices bacon fried and diced

2 tablespoons grated cheese
¼ cup crushed potatoes
1 cup breadcrumbs

Mix first three ingredients in a casserole. Top with breadcrumbs, cheese and potatoes. Bake for about 35 minutes in a moderate oven.

31

FRUITY CALLALOO

1 bunch callaloo,chopped   * salt, pepper
1 cup grapefruit juice

Wash and prepare callaloo,add salt and pepper. Put into a pot with grapefruit juic
Cook quickly for 10 minutes. Drain, correct seasoning and serve.

CARROT AMBROSIA

12 carrots   2 tablespoons sugar
2 tablespoons butter or margarine   2 sliced oranges

Glaze 12 small carrots by melting the sugar and butter in a pan and turning the carro
either sliced or whole, in the mixture over a moderate heat till golden brown.
Add 2 sliced oranges and reheat to serve.

MINT GLAZED CARROTS

12 small carrots (pre-cooked)   1 teaspoon mint sauce
¼ cup butter   ¼ cup sugar

Simmer carrots in the butter. Add mint sauce and sugar. Cook until sugar has melte

CAULIFLOWER CUSTARD

1 cauliflower   1 cup milk
2 eggs   * salt, nutmeg, garlic powder

Boil cauliflower in some salt and water. When cool, break off flowerets and put int
greased dish.
Beat 2 eggs with milk and garlic powder. Pour over cauliflower. Sprinkle with nutm
Bake until set.

CHOCHOS BAKED WITH CHEESE

3 chochos, boiled and sliced   * dabs of butter or margarine
½ cup grated cheese

Place chocho slices in a casserole, in alternate layers with grated cheese and dabs
butter, ending with cheese. Bake until cheese has melted and is crisp on top.

ACKEE SOUFFLE

dozen ackees	4 eggs, separated
tablespoons butter	1 oz. cheese, grated
tablespoons flour	* salt
cup milk	* pepper
	1 teaspoon Worcestershire sauce

Prepare ackees by discarding seeds and taking out pink skin. Wash in salt water. Boil quickly and crush.

In a heavy saucepan, melt the butter and stir in flour. Cook for one minute then add the milk gradually, stirring steadily. Continue cooking and stirring until the mixture thickens then add the salt, pepper and Worcestershire sauce. Remove from heat and allow to cool a little.

Stir in the grated cheese then beat in the egg yolks one by one. Add the crushed ackee and allow the mixture to cool to room temperature.

Preheat the oven to 375°. Butter a 2½ pint souffle dish or fireproof casserole.

Beat the egg whites until stiff. Mix one quarter of the whites into the ackee mixture, then fold in the rest. Pour into the prepared dish and bake in the middle of the oven for 30 minutes when the souffle should be well risen and firm. Serve immediately.

FRIED ACKEES

dozen ackees (or more)	* butter
salt water	

Prepare ackees by discarding seeds and taking out pink skin. Cover in salt water for five minutes. Drain.

Fry in hot butter. Drain on paper towels and serve.

This recipe can be used for tinned ackees.

BEETS WITH ORANGE SAUCE

beets (about 1½ lbs.)	¼ cup orange juice
tablespoons sugar	1 tablespoon lime juice
tablespoon cornstarch	½ teaspoonful grated orange rind
teaspoon salt	1 tablespoon butter

Boil beets in salted water until tender. Drain, reserving the water. Peel the beets and dice.

Combine sugar, cornstarch and salt in the top of a double boiler. Gently stir in ¼ cup of liquid from the cooked beets and the orange juice. Cook over boiling water until thick and smooth, stirring constantly.

Remove from the heat. Stir in remaining ingredients. Add the diced beets and mix lightly. Keep warm over hot water until ready to serve.

STUFFED CHOCHO OR SQUASH

3 chochos or 1 small squash
9 tablespoons minced beef
6 tablespoons bread crumbs
1 tablespoon margarine

1 minced onion
* salt, pepper, oil
* grated cheese

Cut chochos or squash in half and boil until tender but firm. Scrape out the inside a dice, being careful not to break the skin. Saute onions and minced beef in oil and a diced chocho or squash. Fill shells, top with breadcrumbs and a sprinkle of cheese. Ba in 350° oven until brown on top.

CORN FRITTERS

1 tin corn kernels
1 cup milk
1 tablespoon flour

4 tablespoons margarine or butter
* pinch of salt

Make a batter of milk, flour and salt. Fold in whole corn kernels and drop by spoo fuls into bubbling butter or margarine. Fry on both sides.

EGG PLANT (Garden Egg) with
CHEESE AND TOMATOES

2 large eggplants
2 sliced onions
2 sliced tomatoes
1 cup grated cheese

1½ cups water
2 tablespoons oil
* salt, pepper and mixed herbs

Peel and slice eggplant. Sprinkle with salt and let stand for 30 minutes. Wash off s and squeeze dry.

Fry in oil, adding onions and tomatoes. Arrange in layers with cheese in a casserc Add water and seasonings. Bake 45 minutes in a moderate oven.

FOO FOO

green unpeeled bananas
salt and pepper to taste

* water as needed

(This is a well known African dumpling made with starchy foods such as green bananas, green plantains and sometimes mixed with cornmeal and seasoned. Here is a recipe om Barbados.)

Boil bananas, peel, then pound in a mortar. When fruit forms a paste, season with salt d pepper. Mould into balls and reheat in the oven, or drop into boiling water to reheat. rves 4.

OKRA WITH TOMATOES

2 boiled okras
chopped tomatoes
tablespoons breadcrumbs
oz. butter

1 oz. flour
½ pt. milk
* salt, pepper, thyme

Melt butter, stir in flour for 2 minutes. Remove from heat and add the milk gradually. eason and cook over low heat for 5 minutes.

Chop okras, mix with tomatoes and 2 tablespoons of the breadcrumbs. Turn into a aking dish and pour flour-milk mixture over this.

Sprinkle with remaining breadcrumbs and bake for about 15 minutes in a moderate ven.

PEAS AND RICE

cup red peas (soaked overnight)
qrts. hot water
slice salt pork or beef
cups rice
salt

1 sprig thyme
1 grated coconut
1 tablespoon oil
* a piece of hot pepper

Brown onion with salt pork and seasoning. Meanwhile, add 1 cup hot water to grated coconut and squeeze out cream.

Place peas in a pot with 2 quarts water and cook until tender. Add salt pork and asonings and cook for ten minutes. Add rice and cook over low heat until ready. Add ot water if more liquid is needed.

STUFFED PAWPAW (PAPAYA)

1 green pawpaw (just streaked with
   yellow)
2 onions
2 cloves garlic
2 tomatoes
2 slices of ham or bacon

1 sweet pepper
1 hot pepper
1 tablespoon breadcrumbs
1 egg
* salt

Wash pawpaw. Cut off end and scoop out seeds. Chop onions, garlic, peppers and to-matoes and stew for 20 minutes.

Grill bacon and dice. Mix with breadcrumbs, egg and salt. Add to the vegetable ste and pack into pawpaw.

Cover with foil and set in a pan with a cup of water to bake in a moderate oven for a hour. Skin should not be eaten.

BAKED SWEET POTATO

Allow ½ potato per person
3 baked potatoes in skin
2 tablespoons grated coconut

3 tablespoons Red Stripe Beer
2 ozs. butter
* salt, cinnamon

· Cut potatoes in half, scoop out pulp. Crush with beer and butter. Add coconut an salt. Sprinkle with cinnamon and bake through to heat and serve.

PUMPKIN PUFF

2 cups hot mashed pumpkin
2 tablespoons butter
2 tablespoons minced onion
¼ cup milk

1 egg beaten
2 tablespoons flour
* a tip of baking powder
* salt, pepper

Heat oven to 400°. Combine all ingredients and bake in a casserole for 30 minute

---

YAM CASSEROLE

Yellow yam boiled and sliced
3 hard boiled eggs
½ cup grated cheese

1 cup white sauce
* salt, pepper

Place slices of yam alternately with sliced eggs and cheese in a casserole. Sprinkle wi salt and pepper.

Make a white sauce and moisten yam mixture with 1 cup or more. Bake in a modera oven till cheese is melted.

Salads

ACKEE SALAD

cups boiled ackees
chopped, hard boiled eggs

* a few strips of cooked chicken

Prepare ackees and boil for 1 minute. Turn into a colander and run cold water over the ackees, which must be firm.
Mix with chopped hard boiled eggs and strips of chicken. Season to taste.

AVOCADO AND GRAPEFRUIT

avocados
grapefruits
dessertspoon oil

1 dessertspoon vinegar
* salt to taste

Peel and remove seeds from avocados. Slice in circles. Place in individual plates. Fill entres with grapefruit segments. Cover with dressing of oil and vinegar.

BROAD BEAN SALAD

lb. broad beans (shelled)
lb. potatoes
hard boiled eggs

1 tablespoon diced sour pickles
* salt, pepper, oil and vinegar

Boil the beans in some salted water. Boil potatoes. Mix beans, diced potatoes, chopped eggs and pickles and season to taste. Moisten with oil and vinegar.

THREE-BEAN SALAD

1 cup cooked string beans
1 cup cooked red beans or peas
1 cup cooked broad beans
½ cup vinegar

¼ cup oil
½ onion finely chopped
* chopped mint leaves
* a pinch of sugar and salt

Mix beans together and toss with the last five ingredients.

STRING BEAN SALAD

½ lb. cooked beans
1 dessertspoon oil
1 dessertspoon vinegar

½ chopped onion
* a few peanuts

Boil beans in salted water. Drain and dry in a cloth. Serve with oil and vinegar dressi
and some chopped peanuts and onions.

BREADFRUIT SALAD

1 breadfruit
2 hardboiled eggs

* mayonnaise, salt, pepper
* a chopped shallot or small onion

Peel, dice, and boil breadfruit till just firm. Combine with eggs, shallot, salt and peppe
Moisten with mayonnaise.

CALLALOO SALAD

1 lb. callaloo or spinach
6 boiled, sliced potatoes
6 thin slices of cheese

½ cup mayonnaise
* squeeze of lime juice

Plunge callaloo into boiling water for 3 minutes. Drain and chop.
Mix with cold sliced potatoes and thin slices of cheese. Dress with mayonnaise
which is added a squeeze of lime juice.

CARROT AND RAISIN SALAD

6 large carrots
½ cup raisins

* oil and vinegar
* lettuce or cabbage leaves

Shred carrots, mix with raisins and sprinkle with oil and vinegar. Serve on leave

CHICKEN SALAD

2 lbs. chicken
2 cups diced pineapple
3 hard boiled eggs
1 cup green peas

½ cup mayonnaise
1 dessertspoon minced parsley
* salt

Boil chicken, remove the meat and chill. When chilled mix with pineapple, peas, salt and parsley, and toss with mayonnaise. Finally, crumble in the yolks and garnish with egg whites.

CHOCHO SALAD

chochos, peeled, sliced and boiled
sliced onions

* oil and vinegar
* salt and pepper

Place chochos in a shallow dish. Sprinkle with pepper, salt, oil and vinegar. Cover with sliced onions and some more of the oil and vinegar.

BAHAMIAN CONCH SALAD

2 young queen conch
hot peppers
cup vinegar

¼ cup oil
2 sliced onions
* salt
* lime juice

Cover conch with water and bring to a boil, by which time it should be easy to remove the meat. Wash with lime juice and clean.
Dice and mix with chopped hot peppers, vinegar, oil, sliced onions and salt. This is a popular salad in the Bahamas.

CUCUMBER AND SOUR CREAM SALAD

cup sour cream
teaspoon vinegar
tablespoon chopped mint

* a pinch of sugar
* sliced cucumbers

Mix together sour cream, vinegar, mint and sugar. Pour this over the sliced cucumbers. Marinate for an hour before serving.

JAMAICAN SALAD

1 cup freshly grated coconut
2 cups finely shredded cabbage
1 cup pineapple cubes

1 cup mayonnaise
* lettuce leaves

Combine coconut, cabbage and pineapple with mayonnaise mixing well. Chill and serve on lettuce leaves.

LOBSTER SALAD

1 cup mayonnaise
1 teaspoon onion powder
* lobster meat
* dressing

1 dessertspoon creole sauce
* shredded lettuce
* a few drops of lime juice

For each person arrange shredded lettuce on a plate. Top with a helping of lobster meat which has been tossed with the dressing below. Decorate with olives and strips of celery.

ONION SALAD

12 small onions
2 chopped tomatoes
* a handful of currants or raisins

* salt – parsley
* oil and vinegar to taste

Peel and boil onions in a small amount of salted water. When cooked add tomatoes, oil vinegar, parsley and currants. Serve cold.

SWEET PEPPER SALAD

2 red sweet peppers
2 green sweet peppers

2 tablespoons oil
* oil and vinegar to taste

Cut and slice peppers. Take out veins and seeds. Saute quickly in oil. Drain.
Add oil and vinegar with a pinch of salt.

POTATO SALAD

A golden rule is that this must be made whilst potatoes are still hot).

boiled diced potatoes
diced onion
tablespoon flour
tablespoon vinegar
teaspoon sugar

1 tablespoon chopped parsley
6 boiled and sliced frankfurters
   (or vienna sausage)
2 tablespoons oil
* salt, pepper

Fry frankfurters with onion in some oil. Add 1 tablespoon flour and blend. Add sugar, vinegar, parsley, salt and pepper. Mix together well and pour over the potatoes. Toss lightly.

PUMPKIN SALAD

pumpkin, peeled and boiled
teaspoon mixed herbs
tablespoon oil

1 dessertspoon vinegar
* a few lettuce leaves

Place slices of firm boiled pumpkin on lettuce leaves. Make a dressing of herbs and oil and pour over pumpkin.

RICE OR MAÇARONI SALAD

cups cold cooked rice or macaroni
ozs. lean ham
stalks escallion

1 tomato
4 slices cucumber
* herbs

Mix diced vegetables and rice with herbs and ham. Pour dressing over salad.

DRESSING

dessertspoon oil
dessertspoon vinegar
teaspoon soya sauce

1 teaspoon juice from mango chutney
* a squeeze of lime — salt

Mix well together.

SHRIMP SALAD WITH COCONUT CREAM

1 cup milk
1 cup grated coconut
1 tablespoon oil
1 teaspoon salt
2 minced shallots

2 chopped sweet peppers·
2 tablespoons soya sauce
1 tablespoon chopped peanuts
2 lbs. shrimp (cooked and peeled)

Combine milk and coconut in saucepan and bring to boil. Remove from heat and soak for 30 minutes. Press through a sieve to extract cream. Discard pulp.

Heat oil, and fry the shallots and peppers. Remove from heat. Add soya sauce and peanuts. Combine with coconut cream.

Arrange shrimps on a dish and pour dressing over them. Reserve a few shrimps for decoration and chill slightly to serve.

SALAD CREOLE

2/3 pineapple
1/3 of a tomato per person
½ cup fresh cream
1 tablespoon ketchup

* pinch of salt
* squeeze of lime juice
* chopped onion

Cut pineapple into thin strips and dice tomato. Combine next 4 ingredients and pour over salad. Serve on lettuce leaves and top with a sprinkle of chopped onions.

TROPICAL SALAD

1 cup grated coconut
1 cup diced pineapple

1 cup seeded tangerine segments
1 cup mayonnaise

Combine ingredients and serve on cabbage leaves or lettuce leaves.

42

Dressings & Sauces

COOKED SALAD DRESSING

ozs. butter
beaten egg
cup milk
cup sugar

1   teaspoon dry mustard
¼   cup vinegar
*   pinch of salt

Melt butter. Add egg and milk and stir in sugar, salt and mustard, which have been
nded with some vinegar.
Gradually add the rest of vinegar. Stir over low heat in a double boiler until thickened.
not allow to boil. Cool and refrigerate.

HONEY DRESSING FOR FRUIT SALADS

cup vinegar
tablespoons honey

½   cup lime juice
3   tablespoons crushed pineapple

Mix together and chill.

A BASIC WHITE SAUCE

Melt 2 tablespoons margarine on low heat. Add ½ cup flour slowly, whilst stirring,
th 1 cup of milk, and a pinch of salt until this thickens.
Do not allow to burn.

A HOT DRESSING

cup peanut butter
cup tomato ketchup

¼   cup milk
*   a few drops hot sauce

Mix to a paste adding more milk if needed. Use over onions, cucumbers or sweet
ppers.

OIL AND VINEGAR

¼ cup oil
1/6 cup vinegar

1 dessertspoon dry mustard
* pinch of salt

Mix well together.

MY SALAD DRESSING

¼ cup vinegar
2 teaspoons sugar

1 teaspoon mint jelly
* a squeeze of lime and a pinch of sa

Blend together and chill.

A DRESSING FOR SEA FOOD

4 tablespoons mayonnaise
4 tablespoons french dressing
2 tablespoons mango chutney

1 teaspoon lime juice
* a pinch of curry powder
* salt and pepper to taste

Combine and mix all ingredients.

SPICY DRESSING

3 tablespoons vinegar
2 tablespoons sugar

1 tablespoon powdered ginger

Blend together and chill. Delicious on crisp green salad.

2 MINUTE MAYONNAISE

1 teaspoon sugar
½ teaspoon salt
¼ teaspoon dry mustard

½ cup evaporated milk
½ cup oil
2 tablespoons vinegar

Mix all ingredients except oil and vinegar. Add oil gradually in a thin stream and bea
well. Finally, add vinegar slowly, continuing to beat till smooth.

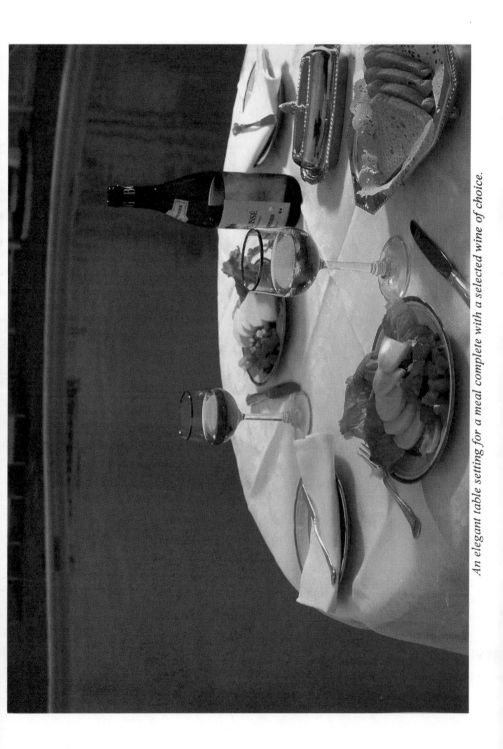

An elegant table setting for a meal complete with a selected wine of choice.

Prawns is a favourite seafood in Caribbean Cuisine.

DEVILS SAUCE

tablespoons brown sugar
dessertspoon creole sauce
tablespoon ketchup
teaspoon hot sauce

1 tablespoon guava jelly
¼ teaspoon salt
3 tablespoons vinegar

Mix all ingredients together in a saucepan and simmer for 2 minutes. Cool and chill.

EGG SAUCE

pt. evaporated milk
eggs
teaspoon vinegar

1 teaspoon lime juice
½ teaspoon pepper and salt

Hard boil eggs and chop. Mix with milk and other ingredients. Excellent over salads.

HOT PEPPER SAUCE

hot peppers
teaspoon oil
teaspoon creole sauce

1 teaspoon ketchup
1 teaspoon vinegar
* salt to taste

Put peppers, and other ingredients through a blender or mincer. Bottle. Makes 1 bottle.

MARINA SAUCE

cup oil
clove crushed garlic
teaspoons minced parsley

3 cups diced tomatoes
1 chopped sweet pepper
* salt to taste

Mix well together and simmer slowly for 30 minutes. Cool and chill.

MARMALADE SAUCE

teaspoons dry mustard
marmalade to taste

2 teaspoons rum
* soya sauce

Mix mustard with some rum to make a paste. Add marmalade and a few drops of soya uce. Serve with barbecued dishes.

PEANUT SAUCE

2 cups crushed peanuts	3 cups water
1 tablespoon chopped onion	2 teaspoons curry powder
3 tomatoes	* salt
1 tablespoon fat	

Put nuts into salted water and boil for 15 minutes. Fry onions and tomatoes and add
to peanut mixture with curry powder. Simmer for about 20 minutes, stirring frequently

---

PEPPERMINT SAUCE

2 egg whites	1 tablespoon sugar
2 cups thin cream (evaporated milk)	2 tablespoons creme de menthe

Beat egg whites stiff. Fold in cream, sugar and creme de menthe. Good over a frui
salad.

RUM SAUCE

4 ozs. butter	2 tablespoons rum
2 ozs. granulated sugar	

Cream butter and sugar and add rum very slowly. Beat well and keep cool.

SABAYON SAUCE

4 ozs. sugar	3 egg yolks
2 tablespoons sherry	* few drops vanilla

Cream sugar and yolks together over a gentle heat. Add vanilla. Gradually add sherr
and whisk vigorously until frothy and firm. Use immediately.

SWEET AND SOUR SAUCE

6 chopped shallots	1½ cups pineapple juice
2 tablespoons vinegar	1 teaspoon soya sauce
1½ tablespoons brown sugar	½ cup water
½ teaspoon ketchup	3 teaspoons cornstarch

Mix all ingredients except water and cornstarch and simmer gently for about 40 min
utes. Mix cornstarch with water and add to the sauce. Simmer 5 minutes more, stirrin
until sauce thickens

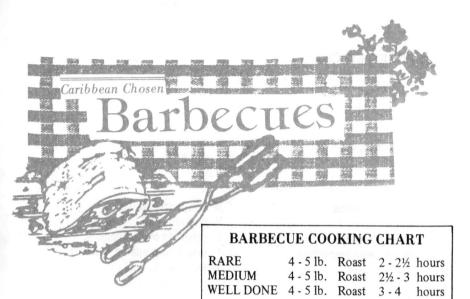

Caribbean Chosen

Barbecues

BARBECUE COOKING CHART				
RARE	4 - 5 lb.	Roast	2 - 2½	hours
MEDIUM	4 - 5 lb.	Roast	2½ - 3	hours
WELL DONE	4 - 5 lb.	Roast	3 - 4	hours

BACON-WRAPPED FRANKFURTERS

lb. frankfurters
ozs. cheddar cheese, sliced

8 rashers bacon
4 teaspoons mustard

Barbecue the frankfurters over medium coals for about 15 minutes, then slice them
gthways, almost through. Fill with cheese slices and press the frankfurters together
in.
Spread the rashers of bacon with mustard and wrap around the frankfurters, securing
ends with wooden cocktail sticks. Place on the grill again and cook over medium coals
a further 5 minutes, or until cheese melts and bacon is crisp. Serve with a mixed green
d and potato chips
Serves 4.

BAKED RED SNAPPER IN
SAVOURY BARBECUE SAUCE

3 lb. red snapper
tablespoons butter
cup chopped onions
cups chopped celery
cup chopped green peppers
cups canned tomatoes
tablespoon Worchestershire/
Pickapeppa sauce

1 tablespoon ketchup
1 teaspoon chili powder
½ lemon, finely sliced
1 teaspoon salt
2 bay leaves
2 teaspoons sugar
1 red pepper

reheat oven to 350oF. Dredge snapper inside and out with seasoned flour. Place in
king pan. In a pot, melt butter. Add onions, celery and green peppers. Simmer until
ry is tender. Add other remaining ingredients and simmer 15 minutes. Pour sauce
r the fish. Bake approximately 45 minutes, basting frequently.
erves 4–5 people.

BARBECUED CHICKEN

1 2½ lb. chicken, cut in serving pieces
* black pepper

* salt to taste
* garlic

SAUCE
¼ cup chopped onions
½ cup water
2 tablespoons vinegar
1 tablespoon Worchestershire/
  Pickapeppa sauce
¼ cup lemon juice
2 tablespoons sugar
1 cup chili/tomato sauce

¼ teaspoon paprika
½ teaspoon salt
1 teaspoon black pepper
1 teaspoon prepared mustard
1 teaspoon ketchup
1 tablespoon butter
* hot pepper sauce to taste

Season chicken liberally with salt, black pepper, garlic. Let stand 1 hour.
To prepare sauce: Saute onions till brown. Add other sauce ingredients and simm
15 minutes, then cool. Broil chicken. Add sauce when chicken is nearly done (after abo
1 hour), basting continually. Serves 4.

BARBECUED CHICKEN WINGS

2 lbs. chicken wings
3 tablespoons honey
3 tablespoons vinegar
2 tablespoons sugar
3 tablespoons soy sauce

1 large clove garlic, crushed
1 stock cube
¼ pint hot water
1 tablespoon sherry

Cut and trim chicken wings. Place in a bowl. Blend together honey, vinegar, sugar, s
sauce and garlic, and pour over the meat. Dissolve stock cube in the hot water, then a
the sherry. Add to the other ingredients in the bowl and stir together. Leave to marina
for 8 to 12 hours or overnight in the refrigerator. Preheat the oven to moderately slow
335°F. Arrange chicken wings on a rack in a roast pan and baste well with the marina
Bake, uncovered, until golden brown, basting occasionally with the sauce, turning or
during the cooking time.
If served as a party-time snack, eat with fingers and provide a finger bowl of wa
water and serviettes to wipe fingers.

BARBECUED CHICKEN
WITH SPECIAL SAUCE

3 lb. chicken
cup tomato sauce or ketchup
teaspoon creole sauce
tablespoon vinegar

1   teaspoon dry mustard
1   teaspoon sugar
*   a drop or two of hot sauce

Cut chicken into pieces. Season with salt and pepper and grill over hot coals basting
frequently with sauce made by combining last 6 ingredients and bringing them to a boil.

BARBECUED LAMB CHOPS

lbs. lamb chops
teaspoon prepared mustard
piece ginger, beaten
medium-sized onions, sliced
tablespoon salad oil
cup water
salt to taste

2   tablespoons chili/tomato sauce
1   tablespoon Worchestershire/
     Pickapeppa sauce
1   tablespoon vinegar
*   hot pepper sauce to taste
*   black pepper

Season chops with mustard, ginger, salt and pepper. Place sliced onions over chops in
aking pan. Combine other ingredients and pour over onions and chops. Bake, covered,
1 moderate oven, basting frequently, for approximately 15-20 minutes or until done.
Remove lid 10 minutes before chops are cooked.
    Serves 6.

BARBECUED MEAT BALLS

1 lb. ground beef
2 tablespoons chopped parsley
1 tablespoon bread crumbs
1 teaspoon salt
½ large onion
1 sprig thyme, chopped

1 egg yolk
1 tablespoon soft butter
1 teaspoon lemon juice
1 teaspoon black pepper
1 small sweet pepper
2 whole pimento grains

SAUCE

1 large sweet pepper
1 clove garlic
1 cup ketchup
1 teaspoon vinegar
1 piece ginger

1 large onion
1 carrot (cut up
   in long strips)
2 tablespoons sugar
½ teaspoon salt (to taste)

To prepare sauce: saute sweet pepper, onion, garlic, carrot in butter. Add other ingredients, then simmer for 20 minutes. Meanwhile, combine meatball ingredients, mold into balls. Skewer balls and place over flame, turning and basting continually with sauce.
Serves 4.

BARBECUED ORIENTAL CHICKEN

1 cup soy sauce
1 cup sake (Japanese rice wine) or
   1 cup grapefruit juice or 1 cup
   dry sherry
¼ cup cooking oil

1 teaspoon sugar
½ teaspoon grated fresh ginger root,
   or ground ginger
* one 2½ pound chicken, cut up

Mix together soy sauce, sake or grapefruit juice or sherry, sugar and ginger in a large shallow dish. Add chicken, turning to coat both sides. Cover and marinate in refrigerator several hours or overnight, turning occasionally. Remove chicken from marinade and brush with oil. Grill about 6 inches from source of heat, brushing with marinade and turning frequently until brown and tender.
Serves 4.

BARBECUED PERCH

5 lb. perch
1 cup celery
1 cup onions
1 cup ketchup
1 tablespoon prepared mustard

1 tablespoon Worchestershire/
   Pickapeppa sauce
2 tablespoons vinegar
2 tablespoons sugar

Grill fish for 10 minutes. Meanwhile, sautee celery and onions. Combine other ingredients, bring to a boil. Baste fish with sauce, cooking for another 10 minutes.
Serves 6-8.

BARBECUED SPARERIBS
(BAKED)

Please use the American style pork spareribs for this succulent recipe. If you can do ⁖e ribs over a good bed of charcoal, attending carefully to the basting, so much the ⁖tter!

to 6 lb. spareribs cut in serving pieces	2 tablespoons lemon juice
lemon thinly sliced	1 teaspoon chili powder
cup molasses	1 tablespoon celery seed
cup prepared mustard	2 tablespoons Pickapeppa sauce
tablespoons vinegar	½ cup tomato ketchup
salt to taste	

Place spareribs, meat side up, in a shallow pan. Sprinkle with salt. Top with lemon ⁖ces.
Bake in a moderate oven 350°F for 30 minutes.
Combine remaining ingredients and blend well. Remove lemon slices. Brush spareribs ⁖th mixture; turn and continue baking one hour longer, basting frequently.
Serve hot.

BARBECUED SPARE RIBS

lbs. spare ribs, cut in serving pieces	¼ oz. garlic powder
teaspoons salt	¼ oz. onion powder
pimento grains, crushed	½ cup paprika
oregano	¼ cup lemon juice
SAUCE	
cup chopped onions	2 tablespoons brown sugar
tablespoon fat	½ cup chili/tomato sauce
cup water	½ teaspoon paprika
tablespoons vinegar	1 teaspoon black pepper
tablespoon Worchestershire/	1 teaspoon prepared mustard
Pickapeppa sauce	* hot pepper sauce to taste

Season ribs with mixture of salt, oregano, garlic, onion and paprika. Rub in to meat ⁖ll. Place ribs in moderate oven with a small amount of water, and cover. Cook for ⁖proximately ½ hour until almost tender. Remove from oven and cool. Place ribs on ⁖k over coals, and turn continually until done (approximately 10 minutes). Make sauce ⁖ combining all ingredients and simmering for 10 minutes. Just a few minutes before ⁖noving from rack, brush ribs with sauce.
Serves 4.

BARBECUED STANDING RIBS (BEEF)

8 10 lbs. ribs
* salt

* black pepper
* garlic powder

SAUCE

14 ozs. ketchup
½ cup white vinegar
1 teaspoon sugar
1/8 teaspoon salt
½ teaspoon cumin

1 teaspoon coriander
1/8 teaspoon paprika
1/8 teaspoon saffron
¼ teaspoon ground ginger
1 red pepper, finely chopped

Season ribs liberally with salt, pepper, garlic powder; let stand overnight. When ready to cook, skewer beef, and cook over coals, turning very slowly, for about 2-3 hours. Meanwhile, combine sauce ingredients, simmer 15 minutes. Baste ribs with sauce only 15 minutes before removing from coals.

Serves 15 people.

To add an extra special touch, orange juice can be added to the basting mixture.

BARBECUED STEAK

2–2½ lbs. sirloin steak
8 ozs. olive oil
¼ cup soy sauce
* salt to taste
* black pepper

1 cup tomato sauce
2 tablespoons brown sugar
1 green pepper, cut in chunks
1 onion, sliced

Season steak with salt and pepper. Combine other ingredients, pour over steak. Marinate in refrigerator 4 hours or overnight, turning occasionally. Broil steak.

Serves 4.

BEEF LIVER IN BARBECUE SAUCE

1 lb. beef liver cut in ¼" slices
2 tablespoons butter or margarine
1 cup sliced onions
½ cup green sweet pepper, cut up
1 tablespoon vinegar
* salt and black pepper

1 tablespoon Pickapeppa sauce
1 teaspoon sugar
1 teaspoon prepared mustard
¼ cup tomato ketchup
½ teaspoon hot pepper sauce

Start heating oven to 325°F. Cut liver slices in half crosswise. Place half of slices side by side, in covered, shallow baking dish; sprinkle lightly with salt and pepper. Saute onion and sweet pepper in butter or margarine and arrange half on liver. Mix vinegar with next five ingredients with rest of liver then rest of sauce. Bake uncovered for 10 minutes.

Makes 4 servings. The family will need no encouragement to try this dish.

CHRISTMAS HAM
WITH BARBECUE SAUCE

1 12-15 lbs. ham
1 cup brown sugar

2 tablespoons mustard
1 cup sherry

Preheat oven to 325°F. Bake ham, allowing 25 minutes per pound. When ham is almost done, remove from oven, score, and add cloves. Make a mixture of brown sugar and mustard, then add sherry. Mixture should be like a thick paste. Coat thickly over ham, then bake for another ½ hour.

JIFFY BARBECUE SAUCE

½ cup tomato ketchup
1 teaspoon dry mustard
1 teaspoon hot pepper sauce
2 teaspoons mango chutney

2 teaspoons Pickapeppa Sauce
* liquid from the can of corn & water
   to make ¾ cup

Combine all ingredients and pour over pork chops.

MEAT LOAF WITH BARBECUE SAUCE

LOAF
1½ lbs. ground beef
½ lb. ground lean pork
3 strips bacon, cut in small pieces
½ cup bread crumbs

½ cup tomato juice
2 eggs
2 tablespoons salt
2 tablespoons minced onions

GARNISH
8 bacon strips

* parsley sprigs

SAUCE
2 tablespoons ketchup
¼ teaspoon Worchestershire/
   Pickapeppa sauce

¼ teaspoon chili powder
1 tablespoon minced onion
2 tablespoons vinegar

Combine all loaf ingredients. Shape into individual loaves (makes 8 loaves). Wrap a strip of bacon around each loaf. Simmer sauce ingredients for 15 minutes, then pour over loaves. Bake at 350°F for 45 minutes, basting once or twice during baking.

ORANGE GRILLED FISH

2 lbs. firm white fish

MARINADE

4 tablespoons soy sauce	½ cup orange juice
2 tablespoons tomato ketchup	* grated rind of ½ orange
2 tablespoons chopped parsley	* salt and blackpepper

Cut the fish into 1" pieces. Mix the ingredients for the marinade together, beating wel
Pour over the fish and leave to marinate for 1 hour. Drain the fish and thread on si
skewers. Grill over hot coals for about 8 minutes, then turn and grill for a further 7 mi
utes. Baste with the marinade during cooking.
Serves 6.

SHRIMP WITH COLD BARBECUE SAUCE

2 lbs. fresh shrimp	¼ teaspoon hot pepper sauce
½ cup finely chopped celery	5 tablespoons horseradish
1 stalk skellion	2 tablespoons prepared mustard
6 tablespoons olive oil	¼ teaspoon paprika
3 tablespoons lemon juice	¾ teaspoon salt
¼ cup ketchup	½ teaspoon white pepper
1 clove garlic	

Clean then poach shrimp. To prepare sauce: rub bowl with garlic, then combine othe
ingredients. Marinate shrimp in sauce for an hour. Serve chilled on a bed of lettuc

---

SMOKED PORK CHOPS, BAKED
WITH JIFFY BARBECUE SAUCE

6 smoked pork chops	1 onion, chopped
1 can whole kernel corn	2 tablespoons oil
1 egg, well beaten	1 ounce margarine
1 cup chopped celery	1 green sweet pepper, chopped

Saute celery, onion and sweet green pepper in margarine, and mix with corn & eg
Brown chops lightly in oil, drain and arrange in a casserole. Cover with the corn mixtu
and pour sauce (see P 54) all over. Bake covered at 350°F for one hour. Remove cov
during last 10 minutes.

SPICY ROAST BEEF BARBECUE

Roasted Irish potatoes, when done liberally drenched with butter or margarine, and maybe roasted ears of sweet corn, would be perfect accompaniments. To cool things off, how about a big cabbage slaw, dressed with Mayonnaise, sprinkled with paprika?

(4 - 5) Beef rump roast, rolled and tied	½ teaspoon Pimento
½ cup butter	½ teaspoon coriander
1 cup vinegar	¼ teaspoon chili powder
½ teaspoon dry mustard	1 tablespoon lemon juice
1 tablespoon minced onion	1/3 cup brown sugar
1 tablespoon Pickapeppa Sauce	* salt and pepper to taste

Leave roast at room temperature for at least on hour. Start the fire in the barbecue, and let the charcoal bed burn until charcoal turns ash gray in colour. Tap the gray ash from the coals with fire tongs. After you start the fire, skewer the roast on the spit rod, through the centre of the roast. (If it is not centred properly, the spit will not turn.) Inset holding forks. When the fire is ready, start to brown the roast. While the roast is browning, combine the sauce ingredients in a saucepan, and heat until the butter melts. Makes about 2 cups. When roast is an even brown on all sides start to baste with the sauce, basting every 20 minutes until done. (See Cooking Chart)

BREAD AND BUTTER PICKLES

1 qrt. sliced cucumbers	1 cup sugar
2 sliced onions	½ teaspoon dry mustard
1 sliced green pepper	* pinch of salt
1 chopped clove garlic	* vinegar and spices

Place onions, cucumbers, pepper, garlic and salt in a pan. Cover with ice cubes and le stand for 2 hours. Drain.

Combine other ingredients and pour over onion mixture. Heat to boil for a few min utes only. Seal while still hot in jars. Makes approx. 4 jars.

CORN RELISH

12 young corn ears	2 teaspoons flour
3 peppers (remove seeds)	4 cups vinegar
1½ cups sugar	4 onions
2 tablespoons salt	* mustard to taste

Remove corn from the cob. Put onions and pepper through a mincer and mix with corn. Cover with 3 cups of vinegar.

To remaining cup of vinegar add sugar, salt, flour and mustard to make a paste.

Add this to vegetable mixture and bring to a slow boil for 30 minutes.

Pour into hot jars and seal.

HOT PEPPERS AND SHALLOTS

6 hot peppers
2 cups white vinegar
* shallots to fill 2 jars

1 clove
* salt
* pimento grains

Slice peppers and remove seeds. Peel and wash shallots. Fill jars with shallots and hot pepper slices.
Boil vinegar with spices and salt. Pour over peppers and shallots and seal.

MANGO CHUTNEY

2 ozs. green ginger
2 lbs. brown sugar
1 lb. green mangoes — peel and slice
½ lb. raisins
1 tablespoon soya sauce

1 oz. garlic powder
2 ozs. salt
1 sliced hot pepper
1 sliced onion

Crush the ginger. Mix all ingredients and bring to a boil. Simmer gently until chutney is thick and syrupy. Correct seasoning.

RED DEVIL

6 peppers, seeded and diced
3 diced onions
1 pint vinegar

1 teaspoon nutmeg
* pinch of salt

Put hot peppers and onions through a mincer. Combine with vinegar, nutmeg and salt and bring to a boil.
Bottle when cool.

TO PRESERVE
FRESH TOMATOES

Choose firm, ripe, small tomatoes without blemish. Put them into a jar with a large mouth. Fill jar with oil (corn oil preferably) so that tomatoes are covered with a layer of oil 1" deep. On top of oil pour a little brandy or rum and seal.

PICKLED WATERMELON

2 lbs. sugar
2 quarts water
¼ cup salt
1 pint vinegar
* rind of watermelon

4 cloves
1 piece hot pepper
* pieces of cinnamon stick (or grated nutmeg)

Peel off outer green skin of watermelon and chop the white flesh into pieces. Cover with water and salt and simmer until tender.

Bring remaining ingredients to a boil for 10 minutes. Add tender melon to this and continue to simmer until melon is transparent. Pack in jars. Approx. 4 jars.

VEGETABLE RELISH

6 carrots
1 pepper, seeds removed
2 onions
2 chochos

1 cucumber
6 olives
2 cups water

Chop carrots, peppers, onions, chochos, cucumbers and olives, add water to cover. Bring to a boil to tenderize. Drain.

DRESSING

½ cup oil
1 cup vinegar
2 tablespoon ketchup

1 tablespoon hot pepper sauce
* salt to taste

Mix dressing and bring to a boil. Pour dressing over the vegetables, which have been packed in sterilized jars. Makes 4 jars.

GARLIC VINEGAR

Steep garlic cloves, which have been pricked with a pin, in vinegar for 10 days. Use for salad dressings.

HERB VINEGARS

Various herb vinegars can be made by loosely packing a jar with a combination of herbs and filling with vinegar.
Stand jar in a saucepan of water and bring to a boil slowly. Then allow to cool. After 2 weeks vinegar will be ready for use.

PEPPER WINE

Fill ¾ bottle with either cherry or bird peppers. Fill up with sherry or rum. Allow to stand for about one week before using.

Jellies & Jams

PINEAPPLE JAM

1 pineapple
* sugar

* nutmeg

Peel and grate the pineapple.
To each lb. of pineapple pulp, add ¾ lb. of sugar. Add nutmeg to taste.
Boil and stir until mixture thickens and sugar is melted. Seal in jars whilst hot. Make
approx. 3 jars.

PUMPKIN JAM

3 lbs. pumpkin
2 lbs. sugar
1 lime

1 orange
* salt

Peel and cut pumpkin into slices, then dice and pack in a jar. Add sugar.
Cover and stand for 12 hours. Drain off liquid and boil until syrupy. Add pumpkin
sliced lime and orange. Stir in a pinch of salt. Boil up, and cook until clear.
Seal in jars. Makes approx. 6 jars.

TOMATO JAM

8 tomatoes peeled and chopped
2 tablespoons lime juice
4 cups sugar

2 tablespoons chopped raisins
½ teaspoon all spice

Simmer tomatoes for 10 minutes. Add all ingredients except sugar and bring to a boil.
Add sugar and continue to boil until sugar melts and mixture thickens. Skim and cook

CALF'S FOOT JELLY

calves feet
qrts. cold water
whites and crushed shells of eggs
juice of 3 limes
juice of 1 orange

2 cups sugar
1 pint sherry
½ teaspoon nutmeg
½ cup water

Clean feet well and put into a pan of cold water. Bring slowly to a boil and simmer for
hours. Set aside to cool overnight. In the morning skim jelly from the top and discard
diment on bottom.
Put on heat and melt slowly. Add egg whites beaten to a froth, the crushed shells, nut-
eg, sugar and fruit juices. Boil hard for 20 minutes without stirring.
Add 1 cup of water and let come to a boil again. Reduce heat and let simmer, covered
r about 30 minutes.
Dip a flannel jelly bag into boiling water. Hang it up with a bowl underneath. Pour
ly into bag and let it drip. The bag must not be touched or jelly will cloud.
Turn jelly into a mould. Stir in wine and put in a cool place.

SEA GRAPE JELLY

lbs. sea grapes
pints water

* sugar

Add grapes to water and bring to a boil.Stir with a wooden spoon and crush fruit whilst
rring. Boil about 20 minutes.
Drip through a sieve without stirring. Measure this juice and for every cup of liquid
d an equal amount of sugar. Return sugar and liquid to heat and boil rapidly. Skim.
il until a little tested on a plate will jell.
Pour into jars, and cool before sealing. Makes approx. 4-5 jars.

ORANGE JELLY
AND GUAVA JELLY

lbs. sliced guavas or 7 cups diced
oranges

7 pints water (boil 30 minutes)
* sugar

These are made to the same formula as seagrape jelly (see above).
Strain and measure juice in each instance, and add an equal amount of sugar. Boil until
uid jells — Pour into jars. Makes approx. 4-5 jars.

BLENDER GRAPEFRUIT
MARMALADE

4 grapefruits	5 cups sugar
2 limes	1/8 teaspoon soda
1½ cups water	1 oz. gelatin powder

Lightly peel and seed grapefruit. Chop two and put into a blender with ½ cup wa
Mince. Add soda to this and boil for 30 minutes.

Cut up remaining 2 grapefruits and limes discarding seeds. Add to ½ cup water i
mince in blender. Add this to cooked mixture with rest of water and boil for 30 minu

Add sugar and stir and boil for 10-15 minutes, being careful to stir frequently to av
burning and to melt sugar.

Add dissolved gelatin to marmalade when it has cooled slightly. Should make 4 j

---

ORANGE MARMALADE

4 large seville oranges	* sugar
2 teaspoons salt	

Wash oranges and peel lightly. Cut into quarters, removing pips and pulp. Cover j
and pulp with water and let stand overnight. Slice (or cut with scissors) the peel v
thinly and add a little salt. Cover with water and soak overnight.

The next morning bring peel to a boil and boil until tender. Strain liquid from pips
pulp and add to the fruit mixture. Measure this and add sugar equal to this quant

Boil up again, simmer and stir until sugar melts and liquid thickens. Be careful no
burn, so at this point cook on a low flame.

When mixture jells, skim and remove and pour into jars.

GUAVA CHEESE

* ripe guavas (whatever number desired)	* sugar

Wash guavas, cut in half, cover with water and boil until tender. Rub through a sie
weigh the pulp, and add an equal quantity of sugar.

Boil until mixture shrinks from sides of pot. Stir all the time to prevent burn

When a little dropped into water forms a ball, pour into a shallow dish. Cool and
into squares when firm.

LIME CURD

4 limes grated and juiced	4 ozs. butter
1 lb. granulated sugar	4 eggs. beaten

Combine all ingredients in a double boiler and simmer until sugar dissolves and m
ture is thick. Makes 2 jars.

Desserts

AMBROSIA

ranges peeled and sliced
mall shredded coconut
ablespoons wine

½ cup pomegranate seeds
* sugar

'ile fruit in alternate layers into a bowl, sprinkle with sugar, coconut and wine. End
a layer of pomegranate seeds.

BANANAS IN BATTER

pe bananas
up rum
ablespoon sugar
easpoon lime juice
zs. flour
il

1 oz. sugar
½ oz. butter
9 tablespoon milk
1 teaspoon baking powder
1 egg

eel bananas and cut into thick chunks. Soak in rum, sugar and lime juice.
lix remaining ingredients except the oil. Dip banana chunks into the batter using a
orated spoon. Fry lightly in hot oil.

RIPE BANANA PIE

liced bananas
ackage lime jello – prepared
s per instructions

* cherries
* shredded coconut (optional)

'lace sliced bananas in a prebaked pie shell. Cover with cooked lime jello mixture.
.

BANANA PUDDING

6 ripe crushed bananas	½ lb. sugar
3 tablespoons melted butter	3 beaten egg white
1 glass white wine	* vanilla to taste

Mix all together and beat until smooth. Put into a souffle dish, and bake in a 325° oven until puffy and golden brown on top. Serve at once. The yolk may be used to make a sauce to serve with the pudding. Decorate with cherries and shredded coconut.

CASHEW NUT ICE CREAM

1 cup grape juice	1 qrt. vanilla ice cream
½ cup chopped cashew nuts	* pinch ginger powder

Mix the juice, nuts and ginger into the ice cream. Refreeze for about 2 hours.

COCONUT CREAM PIE

1½ cups milk	1 teaspoon vanilla and a pinch of salt
¾ cup grated coconut	2 cups flour
3 eggs, separated	1 cup margarine
4 tablespoon sugar	4 tablespoons ice water – salt to taste

Heat milk and set aside, beat yolks and add sugar, vanilla, salt and coconut. Stir heated milk and fold in stiffly beaten egg whites.

Mix together flour, margarine, water and salt to form a dough. Roll out and line a pie dish. Prick the bottom. Pour in filling and bake for 50 minutes in a 350° oven.

COCONUT GIZZADAS

1 lb. brown sugar	2 cups flour
¼ pt. water	¼ teaspoon salt
1 grated coconut	¼ cup margarine
½ teaspoon nutmeg	* iced water to blend

Make a syrup of sugar and water. Add coconut and nutmeg. Mix well. Cool and fill pastry shells made as follows.

Mix flour and salt, cut in margarines and water. Roll out and cut into circles. Mould into cases and pinch up edges. Fill with mixture and bake in a 400° oven until pastry shells are golden brown.

COCONUT MOULD

1 tablespoon gelatin powder	3 cups coconut cream
¼ cup warm water	1 tin condensed milk

Dissolve gelatin in warm water. Mix with coconut cream and condensed milk. Heat through to melt gelatin, but do not boil or mixture will curdle. Cool and chill.

---

per person	1 tablespoon black coffee
1 egg	1 tablespoon rum
oz. plain chocolate	

Melt chocolate over low heat.
Separate eggs, reserving whites, beat yolks and stir into melted chocolate mixed with offee and rum. Whip egg whites and fold into mixture.
Put into individual glasses and chill.

DUCKANOO

nearly dry corn on cob ears	½ cup raisins
cup brown sugar	2 tablespoons spice
dry coconut	* salt, ginger powder

Grate corn and coconut. Mix coconut with water to make 2 cups of cream. Add this quid to remaining ingredients to make a paste.
Spoon into squares of banana leaf which have been dipped into boiling water briefly to ake pliable. Tie into parcels.
Place in boiling water and steam for ¾ of an hour.

TROPICAL FRUIT SALAD

ripe pineapple or melon	* brandy, optional
variety of diced fruits, as desired	

Cut off the top of a ripe pineapple or use a melon cut into 2 parts. Scoop out flesh and ix with diced fruits – as many varieties as desired. Toss with 2 tablespoons brandy if sired.
Return to shell and chill. Fresh lychee and mangosteen can be added for a surprise. oth these fruit are obtainable in the Castleton area.

GUAVA MOUSSE

1 cup tinned guava nectar
1 tablespoon gelatin powder

2 tablespoons water
1 cup whipped cream

Dissolve gelatin in water and add to guava nectar. Heat slowly to melt gelatin.
Cool slightly before adding the whipped cream. Set in individual glasses. Chill to serve

---

GUAVA PIE

CRUST
1½ cups flour
2 tablespoons sugar
1¼ teaspoons baking powder

3 tablespoons butter
¾ cup milk
* a pinch of salt

Mix flour, sugar, baking powder and salt. Cut butter into this and blend until mixutr looks like cornmeal. Stir in milk.
Knead on a floured board for 1 minute. Divide dough into 2 balls. Roll out bottor crust, cut and fit into a greased pie dish. Put in filling of guava slices with some syrup
Cover with remaining dough. Brush over with milk and make one or two slits in th pastry. Bake in a 350° oven for about 30 minutes.

FILLING

6 ripe guavas (when in season)
   or use tinned guavas

* water
* sugar

Peel fresh guavas, cut in half and scoop out seeds. Cover with water, add sugar and bo slowly until fruit is tender and a syrup has formed. Fill crust.

LIME PIE

2 egg yolks
4 ozs. condensed milk
¾ cup lime juice
* salt

6 tablespoons sugar
3 egg whites
1 baked pie shell

Beat yolks, stir in milk and add lime juice gradually. Beat well.
Whip egg whites with a pinch of salt and fold into mixture.
Pour into a baked pie shell and cover with meringue made with 3 stiffly beaten e whites and 6 tablespoons sugar.
Bake in a preheated oven for 10 minutes — or until meringue is a golden colou

mammee apple
8" baked pie shell
tablespoons brown sugar

1 cup water
1 tablespoon lime juice
½ teaspoon mixed spices

Make a syrup with sugar, water and lime juice.
Peel and scrape the fruit, slice and simmer gently in the syrup until tender. Fill the
‚-baked crust and sprinkle with spices.
Chill and serve with cream — or coconut cream if desired.

PIE CRUST

ozs. flour
ozs. margarine

* pinch of salt
* cold water

Combine flour, margarine and salt. Add 2-3 tablespoons cold water to make a soft
ugh.
Roll out pastry larger than pie dish. Cut to fit, lapping over dish edge slightly. Cut a
rder and press it around the dampened edges of dish. Bake for ½ hour in 350° oven.
ow to cool before filling.

BOMBAY MANGO FOOL

Bombay mangoes
teaspoons condensed milk
cup light cream

1 teaspoon lime juice
* nutmeg

Peel mangoes, slice flesh off seeds and put through a blender. Add milk, cream, lime
e and nutmeg. Stir well and chill.

BOMBAY MANGO SPECIAL

mango per person

Halve the mangoes and take out the seeds. Fill cavities with vanilla ice cream

NASEBERRY PANCAKES

1 cup milk
1 egg
1 egg yolk
1 tablespoon sugar

4 oz. flour
1 tablespoon butter
5 naseberries

Combine first 6 ingredients to make a batter. Add the naseberries, peeled and crushed. Mix well and drop by spoonfuls onto a hot, greased fry pan. Brown on both sides Serve with butter or syrup.

ORANGE ICE BOX DESSERT

2 cups milk
2 tablespoons cornstarch
1 cup sugar
4 egg yolks
1 tabelspoon gelatin

2 tablespoons cold water
¾ cup orange juice
1 teaspoon orange rind
1 pt. whipped cream
* sponge cake slices

Heat milk in double boiler. Mix cornstarch, sugar and yolks and pour into warm milk. Cook slowly for 10 minutes.

Dissolve gelatin into warm water and add juice and rind. Place in refrigerator to chill and thicken.

Line a spring form pan with slices of sponge cake. Pour mixture over this and chill. Just before serving top with some whipped cream.

ORANGE SORBET

1½ pts. water
5 ozs. sugar
4 oranges

1 lime
1 glass white wine
1 egg white

Bring the sugar and water to a boil, dissolve and reduce.

Add the grated rind of 1 orange, and the juice of 4 oranges and 1 lime. Bring to a boil strain and cool

Semi-freeze. Whisk egg white briskly and add along with wine to mixture. Freeze until mushy and serve in parfait glasses.

OTAHEITE PUDDING

ipe otaheite apples
¾ cup sugar
2 tablespoons butter or margarine

1 teaspoon spice
1 teaspoon baking powder

Peel and slice apples. Sprinkle sugar in a greased dish and dot with butter and spice. Arrange apple slices on top. Pour naseberry batter (see pg. 69) over the slices, or use other batter, adding 1 tsp. of baking powder. Bake at 350° for 35 minutes.

PICKNEY'S SWEET

½ jar of strawberry jam
a little water

* whipped cream and chopped nuts

Heat jam with water to thin slightly. Pour into glasses. Cool and top with whipped cream and chopped nuts.

RUM COFFEE JELLY

2 tablespoons gelatin
2 cups of hot strong coffee
½ cup sugar
2 tablespoons lime juice

3 tablespoons rum
2 cups sour cream
1 cup brown sugar
½ teaspoon cinnamon

Soften gelatin in ½ cup of cold water. Add hot coffee and sugar and stir until gelatin is dissolved. Add lime juice and rum.
Pour into an 8" dish and chill until firm. Cut into cubes and serve a sauce made by beating together sour cream, sugar and cinnamon until sugar dissolves.

A TASTY, LOW-CHOLESTEROL
RECIPE FOR PASTRY

1 cup flour
½ teaspoon salt
¼ cup vegetable oil

2 tablespoons skim milk (use instant) powder mixed in water

Mix flour and salt. Combine oil and milk and pour over flour. Stir with a fork till smooth. Shape into a ball, flatten and wrap with a sheet of waxed paper. Chill. Peel off the paper and roll out. Use as desired.

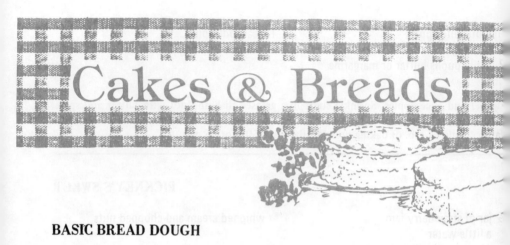

Cakes & Breads

BASIC BREAD DOUGH

2½ cups flour	2 tablespoons melted butter
1 teaspoon dry yeast	5 tablespoons cold milk
½ cup warm water	1 egg beaten into 1 tablespoon milk
* pinch of salt	2 tablespoons flour

Sift flour and salt. Dissolve yeast in ½ cup of warm water. Combine with butter and milk. Cover bowl and set aside to rise for 2 hours.

Put 2 tablespoons flour on table and pat dough to ½" thickness. Cut dough into pieces and roll from corner to corner like a jelly roll.

Brush with egg and milk and slash surface at intervals. Place in bread loaf pans and bake 15 minutes in a fast oven, then lower to 350° and bake 15 minutes more.

BANANA BREAD

1 cup sugar	1 unbeaten egg
¼ cup margarine or butter	1 teaspoon baking powder
3 crushed, ripe bananas	½ teaspoon soda
2 cups flour	* vanilla flavouring

Cream sugar and butter. Add bananas and mix well. Add egg and dry ingredients and vanilla. Beat well.

Bake in a greased, paper lined loaf tin at 350° for 50 minutes. This freezes well.

EGG BREAD

pk. yeast
cups flour
cup warm water
tablespoon oil

2 teaspoons sugar
2 eggs (beaten)
1 egg yolk

Soak yeast in warm water for 5 minutes. Sift flour, salt and sugar together. Add 1½ ups flour to the yeast and beat. Cover and allow to rise about 30 minutes.

Add the 2 eggs and remaining flour and oil to dough. Knead. Place in a bowl to rise for hours.

Knead dough again. Divide into 3 strands and braid, turning ends under. Place on a eased sheet and let rise for 1 hour.

Preheat 400°. Brush the top with egg yolk. Bake for 10-15 minutes. Reduce oven to ;0° and bake 30 minutes. Bread should be golden brown on top.

ORANGE BREAD

cup minced orange peel
cup orange juice
½ cups of sugar
beaten egg
½ cups flour

1 cup milk
½ teaspoon melted butter
2 teaspoons baking powder
* pinch of salt

Combine orange peel and juice and boil until peel is tender. Add 1½ cups sugar, and oil slowly until thick and syrupy. Cool.

Mix egg, 1 cup sugar, butter and milk. Sift flour with baking powder and salt. Add ixture and stir. Add orange mixture to dough and blend well.

Pour into 2 loaf tins which have been greased and floured. Bake at 350° for 40 min÷ tes. This is good toasted with cheese spread.

PUMPKIN BREAD

cups sugar
cup oil
eggs

1 cup boiled, crushed pumpkin
3 cups flour

Grease and flour 2 loaf pans. Mix all ingredients together in a large bowl. Pour into ns.

Bake 1 hour at 350°. Cool for 10 minutes in the pan. Wrap in foil and store in the re- gerator.

SODA BREAD

1 lb. flour
1 cup warm milk

2 tablespoons soda
1 tablespoon salt

Mix all ingredients and knead to a soft dough. Divide into 2 loaves.
Brush with milk and dredge lightly with flour. Bake for 30-40 minutes or until lightly
brown on top in a 425° oven.

BAKING POWDER BISCUITS

2 cups flour
2½ teaspoons baking powder
1/3 cup margarine

¾ cup milk
* salt

Sift together flour and baking powder. Cut margarine into the flour mixture with a
fork. Add milk and salt. Knead and roll out to ½" thickness.
Cut into circles and bake on an ungreased sheet for 15 minutes in a hot oven, 400°
450°.

BANANA MUFFINS

6½ ozs. flour
1 tablespoon corn flour
2 ozs. butter
3 ozs. sugar

1 egg
3 crushed bananas
1 teaspoon baking powder
½ teaspoon soda and a pinch of salt

Sift together, flour, cornflour, baking powder, soda and salt. Cream butter and sugar
Beat egg and mix into creamed mixture.
Add dry ingredients and crushed bananas alternately. Do not beat, but mix in well
Bake in greased muffin containers in 400° oven for 20 minutes.

BAPS

1 lb. flour
½ teaspoon salt
2 ozs. margarine

1 teaspoon sugar
½ pt. of warm milk
2 teaspoons yeast powder

Rub margarine into flour and salt. Dissolve yeast in warm milk and add to the flour
mix along with sugar.
Allow to rise. Punch down, knead and divide into balls and roll out to an oval. Place
on a sheet – dredge with flour and allow to rise again for 30 minutes – bake in a 400°
oven.

BULLAS

3 cups flour　　　　　　　　　1 teaspoon baking powder
8 ozs. brown sugar　　　　　　½ teaspoon soda
2 tablespoons melted butter　　1 teaspoon nutmeg
2 ozs. water　　　　　　　　　½ teaspoon ginger powder

Make a syrup of water and sugar. Sift together dry ingredients and add syrup and melted butter.

Turn on to a floured board and pat into ¼" thickness. Cut into circles. Place on a greased tin and bake for 20 minutes in a 400° oven.

CASSAVA BAMMY

2 lbs. sweet cassavas

Scrape the cassava and grate. Squeeze out the juice, letting the flour remain. Rub through this flour to remove all lumps.

Put a thick-bottomed pan over a low heat and when hot, pour in the cassava flour. When it sets at the bottom, turn over and let the other side set. Scrape to remove any scorching.

Bammies may be moistened with a little milk and baked in a oven or browned under grill, or fry them in a pan with a little bacon fat. Each bammy should be about 5"-6" in diameter and about ½"-¾" thick.

CASSAVA PUFFS

1 lb. sweet cassava　　　　　1 teaspoon baking powder
1 tablespoon margarine　　　1 teaspoon salt
1 beaten egg

Peel cassavas and boil until tender with some salt. Crush whilst still hot.

Add margarine, baking powder and beaten egg and beat.

Drop by spoonfuls into muffin tins which have been greased. Bake for 15 minutes in hot oven.

Puffs may also be fried.

A JAMAICAN BUN

1 lb. flour	6 ozs. currants
2 ozs. butter	½ lb. brown sugar
2 ozs. margarine	½ teaspoon nutmeg
2 ozs. raisins	½ teaspoon baking powder
2 ozs. mixed peel	* enough milk to make a batter
2 eggs	

Blend butter and margarine into flour. Add baking powder, sugar and nutmeg. Add fruit to flour.

Beat the eggs and pour into the dry mixture adding enough milk to make a batter. Pour into a greased loaf tin and bake 1½ hours in a slow oven. about 300°.

Chopped cherries and some lime rind may be added to the mixture if desired.

COCONUT LOAF CAKE

½ cup butter	2 eggs
1½ cups sugar	4 teaspoons baking powder
2 + 2/3 cups flour	1 cup grated coconut
¾ cup milk	1 teaspoon vanilla

Cream butter and ½ of the sugar. Beat eggs with rest of sugar and combine the mixture.

Mix in flour and baking powder adding milk alternately with the dry ingredients. Add coconut and vanilla. Bake 1 hour in a 350° oven.

GUAVA LAYER CAKE

½ lb. margarine	2 teaspoons baking powder
1 cup sugar	¼ teaspoon nutmeg
2 eggs	½ teaspoon vanilla
2 cups flour	* stewed guava slices, or use tinned
1 cup milk	

Cream margarine, sugar and eggs. Beat well. Add flour, baking powder and nutmeg. Pour in milk to which vanilla has been added.

Bake in two 9" layer tins for 30 minutes in a 350° oven. Cool and remove from pans. Spread guava slices between the layers. Sprinkle sugar lightly on top.

Stewed mangoes may be used in the same manner.

74

ORANGE CAKE

3 oranges
2 eggs
¾ cup sugar
2 cups flour

½ teaspoon soda and a tip of salt
1 cup butter
¼ cup grated orange rind

Squeeze juice from oranges to make 1 cup and reserve. Cream butter and sugar and add eggs one at a time, beating continuously.

Add flour, salt and soda, which have been sifted together. Continue to beat the mixture. Add ¼ cup of orange rind and the juice.

Pour into a greased 13" x 9" pan and bake in a moderate oven until firm.

RUM CAKE

½ cup butter
1 cup sugar
3 beaten eggs
¼ teaspoon salt
½ teaspoon baking powder
3 cups flour
* mixed spices

¼ cup milk
¼ cup molasses
2 cups peanuts (crushed)
1 lb. raisins
½ cup rum
* pinch of soda

Cream butter, sugar and eggs. Mix flour, baking powder, salt and spices. Add this to butter mixture and blend.

Add milk, soda and molasses, and add lastly crushed nuts, raisins and rum.
Bake in a loaf tin 300° for 2 hours.

KATIE'S SHORT BREAD

1 oz. sugar
4 ozs. butter

2½ ozs. flour
2½ ozs. cornflour (cornstarch)

Cream butter and sugar. Add flour and cornflour and blend thoroughly.

Put through a cookie tube or drop by spoonfuls onto a greased sheet. Bake for 10 minutes in a 375° oven. Sprinkle with sugar.

COCONUT COOKIES

¾ cup sugar
¼ lb. butter
1½ cups flour

1 tsp. baking powder
1½ cups grated coconut
1 beaten egg

Cream butter and sugar. Add flour and baking powder. Mix well then add grated coco nut and egg.

Mix to a paste. Drop onto a greased cookie sheet by teaspoonfuls. Bake at 350° for 15 minutes. Makes approx. 2 doz.

GUAVA JELLY COOKIES

4 ozs. butter
2 ozs. sugar
1 egg yolk
½ teaspoon vanilla
4 ozs. flour

1 egg white
3 tablespoons chopped nuts
3 tablespoons guava jelly
* pinch of salt

Cream butter and sugar and beat in yolk and vanilla. Combine flour and salt and add to mixture.

Divide and shape into balls. Roll in egg white and then in nuts. Press a hole into each cookie and insert guava jelly.

Bake with jelly uppermost, on a sheet for 20 minutes in a moderate oven. Makes approx. 1 doz.

SWEET POTATO COOKIES

1½ cups flour
2 tablespoons brown sugar
4 teaspoons baking powder
5 tablespoons butter

1 cup crushed, boiled, sweet potato
½ cup of milk
* cinnamon

Combine all but milk and potatoes and mix until crumbly. Stir in crushed potatoes and milk.

Spoon batter on to a sheet.
Bake in a quick oven.
Split and serve with honey and butter. Makes approx. 1 doz.

Beverages

MATRIMONY

| star apples | 4 tablespoons condensed milk |
| oranges | * nutmeg |

Remove starapple pulp. Peel orange and remove sections, discarding seeds.
Mix together, sweeten with condensed milk, and flavour with grated nutmeg. Chill.

NASEBERRY NECTAR

| naseberries peeled and seeded | 1 cup water |
| cup sugar | * juice of 1 orange |

Put all ingredients through a blender, strain and serve chilled.

PLANATION RUM PUNCH

| ozs. any rum | 1 teaspoon honey |
| oz. lime juice | * nutmeg |

Mix together and pour over cracked ice. Add a sprinkle of nutmeg.

SORREL APPETIZER

1 lb. prepared sorrel   6 pints boiling water
2 ozs. grated green ginger

Mix ingredients together, cover and leave overnight. Strain and add rum and sugar t
taste. Serve over crushed ice.

SOURSOP PUNCH

1 ripe soursop   * condensed milk to taste
4 glasses water   * vanilla or rum to flavour

Peel and crush soursop, removing seeds. Stir in water and strain. Add milk and flavou
ing. Serve ice cold.

STARAPPLE APPETIZER

6 star apples(use pulp only)   2 teaspoons lime juice
2 tablespoons rum   * angostura bitters
2 tablespoons sugar

Cut star apples in half, remove pulp and mix with rum, sugar and lime juice. Add a fe
drops of angostura bitters. Serve chilled in fruit glasses.

For a full range of non-alcholic beverages see CARIBBEAN COCKTAILS & MIXED DRINKS
by Mike Henry

BANANA MILK-SHAKE

ripe bananas
pint milk (cold)

1 scoop vanilla ice cream
½ teaspoon vanilla

Puree the bananas in a blender. Add the cold milk, ice cream and vanilla. Blend well nd serve in two tall glasses with straws. If the milk shake is very thick, it can be served ver cracked ice.

CHRISTMAS CITRUS PUNCH

cups grapefruit juice
cups ortanique juice
cups orange juice
bottles soda water

¾ cup honey (or to taste)
1 whole orange, unpeeled
12 cloves

Stick the cloves into the orange and bake in a warm oven until hard.
Put the honey into a large bowl and add the fruit juices gradually, stirring so that ιe honey is completely dissolved. Add the baked orange. Allow the mixture to stand ∙r two hours at least.
When ready to serve, place a block of ice in a large bowl and pour the punch over it. se a ladle to pour the punch over the ice repeatedly until it is completely chilled. Add ιe soda water and serve.
Rum can be added to this punch while it is standing. It can also be garnished with rigs of mint.

JAMAICAN GINGER BEER

lb. root ginger
lbs. sugar
oz. yeast

1 lime
½ oz. cream of tartar
6 quarts boiling water

Grate ginger and place in a large bowl. Add the lime thinly sliced and cream of tartar. ∙ur the boiling water over all and allow to stand.
In a separate bowl, mix yeast with one cup sugar. Add ½ cup luke warm water to ake a smooth paste.
When the ginger mixture is luke warm, add the yeast and sugar. Stir well. Cover. Let ιnd for 2-3 days. Skim and strain, then add the sugar, stirring well until it is dissolved. ∙ur into bottles and let the ginger beer stand at room temperature for three or four ys more. Serve chilled. Rum can be added at the bottling stage, if desired.

Caribbean Chosen

Menus

Brunch

1. Hot Buttered Rum or Carrot Punch *
   Quickie Jerk Pork
   Solomon Gundy
   Banana Muffins
   Mango Fool

2. Boo Boo's Special *
   Curried Codfish
   Fruited Cabbage
   Baps
   Katie's Shortbread
   Coffee a la Mike

3. Policeman Glow *
   Ackee & Saltfish
   Stuffed Breadfruit
   Callaloo Salad
   Matrimony

4. Bloody Mary *
   Escoveitch of Fish (Grouper)
   Bammy
   Naseberry Pancakes served with syrup and butter, or orange jelly
   Jamaican Coffee

5. Coffee Coconut *
   Crab Fritters
   Cucumber and Sour Cream Salad garnished with sweet peppers
   Pumpkin Bread served with tomato jam
   Tropical Fruit Salad

6. Sour-Sop Punch *
   Liver with sweet pepper
   Cassava Puffs served with pineapple jam
   Ambrosia
   Coffee a la Blue Mountain

7. Naked Lady or Hot Barbados Rum Egg Nog*
   Fresh Fruit Plate
   Pepper Shrimps
   Ackee with Cheese
   Jamaican Bun

lunch

1. Hot Flashes*
   Jamaica Fish Pie
   Pumpkin Salad garnished with sweet pepper rings and parsley
   Otaheite Pudding

2. Pineapple Cocktails*
   Jamaica Fish Tea
   Broad Bean Salad
   Beef & Mango in beer
   Yam Casserole
   Sliced Tomatoes
   Orange Sorbet

3. Air Conditioner *
   Jamaica Pepper Pot Soup
   Chicken Salad
   Sweet Pepper Salad
   Pumpkin Bread
   Coconut Mould

4. Banana Punch*
   Coco Soup
   Tropical Chicken   with rice
   String Bean Salad
   Rum Coffee Jelly

5. Woodpecker *
   Jamaican Salad
   Curried Goat with rice
   Mammee Apple Pie

6. Special Jamaican Rum Punch (hot) *
   Fish Chowder
   Poor Man's Fillet
   Rice & Peas
   Carrot & Raisin Salad
   Guava Mousse

7. Spanish Town *
   Pumpkin Soup
   Marinated Pork Chops
   Cho Cho Salad
   Breadfruit Salad
   Coconut Cream Pie

Dinner

1. Desperate Virgin *
   Grapefruit with shrimp & sour cream
   Jamaican Salad
   Conch Soup
   Salmi of Duck
   Pumpkin Puff
   Chochos baked with cheese
   Guava Layer Cake

2. Suffering Bastard *
   or Starapple Appetizer
   Avocado & Grapefruit Salad
   Gungo Pea Soup
   Pork Chops with Pineapple
   Baked Sweet Potatoes
   Coffee Mousse

3. Clarendon Cocktail *
   Ackee Salad
   Red Pea Soup
   Dumperpumpkin with rice
   Onion Salad
   Guava Pie

4. Frozen Daiquiri (Stella's Joy) *
   Lobster Salad
   Barbecued Lamb Chops
   Callaloo Bake
   Mint Glazed Carrots
   Orange Ice Box Dessert

5. Pineapple Caribbean *
   Conch Salad
   Barbecued Chicken
   Corn Fritters
   Cauliflower Custard
   Banana Pudding

6. Dry Martini *
   Shrimp Salad with coconut cream
   Cold Thick Cucumber Soup
   Boned Stuffed Leg of Kid with browned potatoes
   Egg Plant with Cheese & tomatoes
   Carrot Ambrosia
   Ripe banana pie

7. West Indian Punch *
   Tropical Salad
   Cho Cho Puree
   King Fish Fillets
   Yam Casserole
   Beans in sour cream sauce
   Lime Pie

===

* See Caribbean Cocktails by Mike Henry

GLOSSARY OF COOKING TERMS

Bain – Marie A French cooking utensil similar to a double boiler used to cook over boiling water

Bake To cook by dry heat, usually in an oven

Barbecue Generally refers to food cooked outdoors over an open fire with a spicy sauce

Baste To brush or spoon liquid over food while cooking, to keep it moist

Batter Any combination which includes flour, milk, butter, eggs or the like for pancakes, coating, dipping etc.

Beat To mix with a whisk beater or spoon so as to make the mixture smooth

Blanch To heat in boiling water or steam for a short period only to loosen skin, remove colour or set colour

Blend To mix two or more ingredients.thoroughly

Boil To cook in any liquid at boiling point

Bone To remove bones from meat, poultry, game and fish

Chill To place in refrigerator until cold

Coat To cover entire surface of food with flour, bread crumbs, or batter

Cream To combine butter or other shortening with sugar using a wooden spoon or mixer until light and fluffy

Croutons Small cubes of fried bread

Cut in To mix batter or margarine with dry ingredients, with pastry blender, knives or fork

Deep fry To cook in deep hot fat or oil which covers the food until crisp and golden

Dice To cut into small cubes

Disjoint To separate the joints – of poultry etc.

Dot To scatter small bits of butter or margarine over surface of food

Flame To spoon alcoholic fluid over and ignite, to warm the alcohol, and pour flaming over food

Fold in To use a spoon in a gentle rolling circular action as a means of combining ingredients

Fry To cook in hot fat using moderate to high heat

84

Ghee	Clarified butter, used in curries	Puree	To press through a fine sieve or put through a food blender to produce a smooth mixture
Glaze	A thin coating of beaten egg-milk, syrup or aspic which is brushed over pastry, fruits, ham chicken etc.	Reduce	To cook over a high heat, uncovered until it is reduced to desired consistency
Grate	To rub food against a grater to form small particles	Roast	To cook meat by dry heat in the oven or on a spit
Marinade	Liquid used for seasoning by soaking usually a mixture of oil, wine and seasonings	Roux	A mixture of fat and flour cooked slowly, stirring frequently — used to thicken sauces soups etc.
Marinate	To soak in a marinade to soften or add flavour	Salmi	A hash — usually of duck
Parboil	To boil until partly cooked	Saute	To fry lightly in a small amount of fat turning and stirring frequently
Pate	A highly seasoned meat paste		
Pit	To remove pit—stone or seed—from fruit	Scald	To pour boiling water over foods, or bring to boiling.
Poach	To cook gently in simmering liquid	Score	To cut narrow gashes on the surface of foods
Pound	To reduce to small particles or a paste, using a pestle and mortar	Shred	To cut into fine strips
		Simmer	To cook in liquid just below boiling point
Preheat	To turn over to a selected temperature 10 minutes before it is needed	Skim	To remove foam, fat or solid substances from the surface of a cooking mixture.
Grill	To cook by direct heat either over a charcoal fire or under a gas or electric grill unit	Sliver	To cut into long thin strips
		Steam	To cook in vapour rising from boiling water
Julienne	A term for foods cut into thin strips like matches	Stew	A long slow method of cooking in liquid in a covered pan, to tenderize tough meats.
Knead	To work dough with hands until it is of the desired elasticity or consistency	Stir	To blend ingredients with a circular motion

Stock	A liquid containing the flavours, extracts, and nutrients of bones – meat – fish or vegetables, in which they are cooked	Toss	To mix lightly, using a fork and a spoon – i.e. salads chiefly
Toast	To brown in a toaster, or oven	Whip	To beat rapidly with hand or electric beater or wire whisk

---

35 USEFUL COOKING & HOUSEHOLD HINTS

1/3 to 1/2 teaspoon of dried herbs = 1 tablespoon fresh herbs.

Rub ½ lime on your hands or cutting board to remove onion, garlic or fish odours.

To avoid trouble with weevils, keep flour or cornmeal in a glass jar or plastic container in the refrigerator.

1 tablespoon oil in water for boiling pastas (macaroni etc.) prevents it from sticking together.

1 lb. coffee brews 40 cups.

For a tender pie crust use less water than is called for.

Dip knife in hot water to slice hard boiled eggs.

1 cup macaroni makes 2 cups of cooked macaroni.

Freeze left over coffee in an icecube tray. When used to chill iced coffee, the cubes will not dilute the coffee.

Parsley rinsed in hot water instead of cold retains more flavour.

Brown sugar will not become lumpy if stored in a jar with a piece of blotting paper fitted to the inside of the jar lid.

If food boils over in the oven, cover with salt to prevent smoking and excessive odour.

Add diced crisp bacon and a dash of nutmeg to cauliflower or cabbage for a gourmet touch.

To keep kettles clean, fill with cold water, add some ammonia and bring to a boil. Rinse well.

Gas ovens must be wiped clean before oven is cold. Racks and shelves must be washed with hot water and washing soda.

Wash pewter with hot water and soap, polish will scratch the surface.

Mildew stains can be removed by soaking overnight in sour milk. Dry in the sun without rinsing. Repeat process if necessary.

To remove a scorch, spread a paste of starch and cold water over the mark. Dry in sun and brush off.

Wash glass windows with crumpled newspaper dipped in cold water, to which has been added a few drops of ammonia.

For wood worms – apply kerosene oil with a brush to the infected area daily for 10 days.

To stop doors creaking rub hinges with soap.

Rust marks can be removed from steel by rubbing with a cut onion.

When washing thermos flasks, add a little vinegar to the water. It removes the musty smell. Do not cork flasks when storing.

To remove stains from china use a rag dipped in cold water and salt.

Before baking have ingredients at room temperature.

To chop sticky dried fruits, heat knife before using.

To prepare nuts, first blanch. Cover with cold water and bring to the boil. Let soak until skin wrinkles then slip the skin off between the fingers.

Parsley freezes well. Cut stems and place bunch in a plastic bag. Thaws easily.

Tear lettuce into pieces instead of cutting to prevent browning.

It is a good idea to make stock from left over bones and keep in the freezer to enhance soups and sauces.

Soak tarnished silver in hot water and ammonia – 1 tablespoon ammonia to 1 quart water.

Sour milk can be made by adding two teaspoons of lime juice to a cup of warm milk, which will curdle.

Moulds should be oiled before they are filled. Custards baked in hot water should be removed and left to stand for 5 minutes to settle before unmoulding. Run knife around the edge. Place a plate over the mould, invert the plate and mould and lift off.

As soon as vegetables are tender drain and plunge into cold water. This sets the colour. Vegetables may be stored and reheated when needed.

Whip cream in a large bowl set in ice. If no cream is available, place a tin of evaporated milk in the freezer for about one hour and then proceed to whip as for cream. To sweeten, use icing sugar, which is preferable to granulated sugar.

TABLE OF MEASUREMENTS AND MISCELLANEOUS EQUIVALENTS

Dash	=	Less than 1/8 teaspoon
3 teaspoon	=	Tablespoon
4 tablespoons	=	¼ cup
8 tablespoons	=	½ cup
16 tablespoons	=	1 cup
1 cup	=	½ pint
2 cups	=	1 pint
4 cups	=	1 qrt.
2 liquid cups	=	1 lb.
2 pints	=	1 quart
4 quarts	=	1 gallon
1 fluid ounce	=	2 tablespoons
8 fluid ounces	=	1 cup
16 ounces	=	1 pound
1 lb. butter	=	2 cups
1 carrot	=	½ cup chopped
¼ lb. cheese	=	1 cup grated
1 envelope gelatin	=	1 tablespoon
1 teaspoon dried herbs	=	1 tablespoon fresh
juice of 1 lime	=	1 tablespoon
1 medium onion	=	¾ cup chopped
1 medium potato	=	½ cup chopped
1 pk. dry yeast	=	¼ oz.

SOME SUBSTITUTIONS

When you do not have exactly what the recipe calls for, here are some suggestions which are acceptable substitutes.

1 square cooking chocolate	3 tablespoons cocoa + 1 oz. butter
1 cup self raising flour	1 cup plain flour + 2 teaspoons of baking powder
1 cup sour milk	1 tablespoon lime juice or white vinegar 1 cup milk
1 cup fresh milk	½ cup evaporated milk + ½ cup water
1 cup sour cream	1 cup warm milk + 1 tablespoon lime juice or white vinegar. Stirred to a thick consistency
Yeast compressed (1 oz.)	2 Teaspoons active dry yeast
1 fresh garlic clove	¼ teaspoon garlic powder
fresh green root ginger, grated	¼ – ½ teaspoon ground ginger

QUANTITIES PER HEAD

Appetizers	a variety of 4 - 6
Soup	5 servings to 1 quart
Sauces	10 servings to 1 pint
Fish	6 ozs. without bone
	8 ozs. with bone
Meat	4 ozs. without bone
	6 ozs. with bone
Green vegetables	6 servings 8 ozs.
Potatoes	4 servings 8 ozs.
Puddings/cold sweets	3 servings to 1 pint
Ices	10 servings to 1 quart
Poultry (chicken)	6 portions from a 4 lb. chicken
Poussin (chicken 3 - 4 weeks old)	i portion

USEFUL KITCHEN EQUIPMENT

Cake tester	Blender
Poultry shears	Food chopper
Colander	Meat pounder
Rotary egg whisk	Nut grinder
Pastry blender	Pots, pans, casseroles
Pastry brush	Knives
Cheese graters	Sieves, rubber scrapers, bulb basters

Pots must be heavy bottomed. The best all purpose material is undoubtedly heavy enamelled cast iron. Copper pots are very satisfactory — the metal should be 1/8" thick and the handle should be of iron. A kitchen should have round and oval casseroles. Saucepans in various sizes — a skillet (sloping sides) and a saute pan (straight sides).

Omelette Pan — This can be made of iron, with a long handle and a 2" sloping side and a 7" diameter bottom. This is perfect for 2 — 3 egg omelettes. When new, scrub with steel wool and scouring powder. Rinse and dry. Heat it and rub bottom with oil and let it stand overnight. Just before using, sprinkle 1 teaspoon of salt in the pan and rub with a paper towel.

Knives must be good quality, and kept in good condition. A 9" blade for chopping vegetables, a pointed knife for filleting, which should have a 6½" flexible blade. Knives for splitting chickens should have a 12" blade and should be heavy.

A carver should only be used for carving.

INDEX